Villeneuve
Caumont
Myvathen Mire
Wyrm Hill
River Erath
Perrault
The Great Oak
The Enchanted Forest
River Oult
E
N
S
W

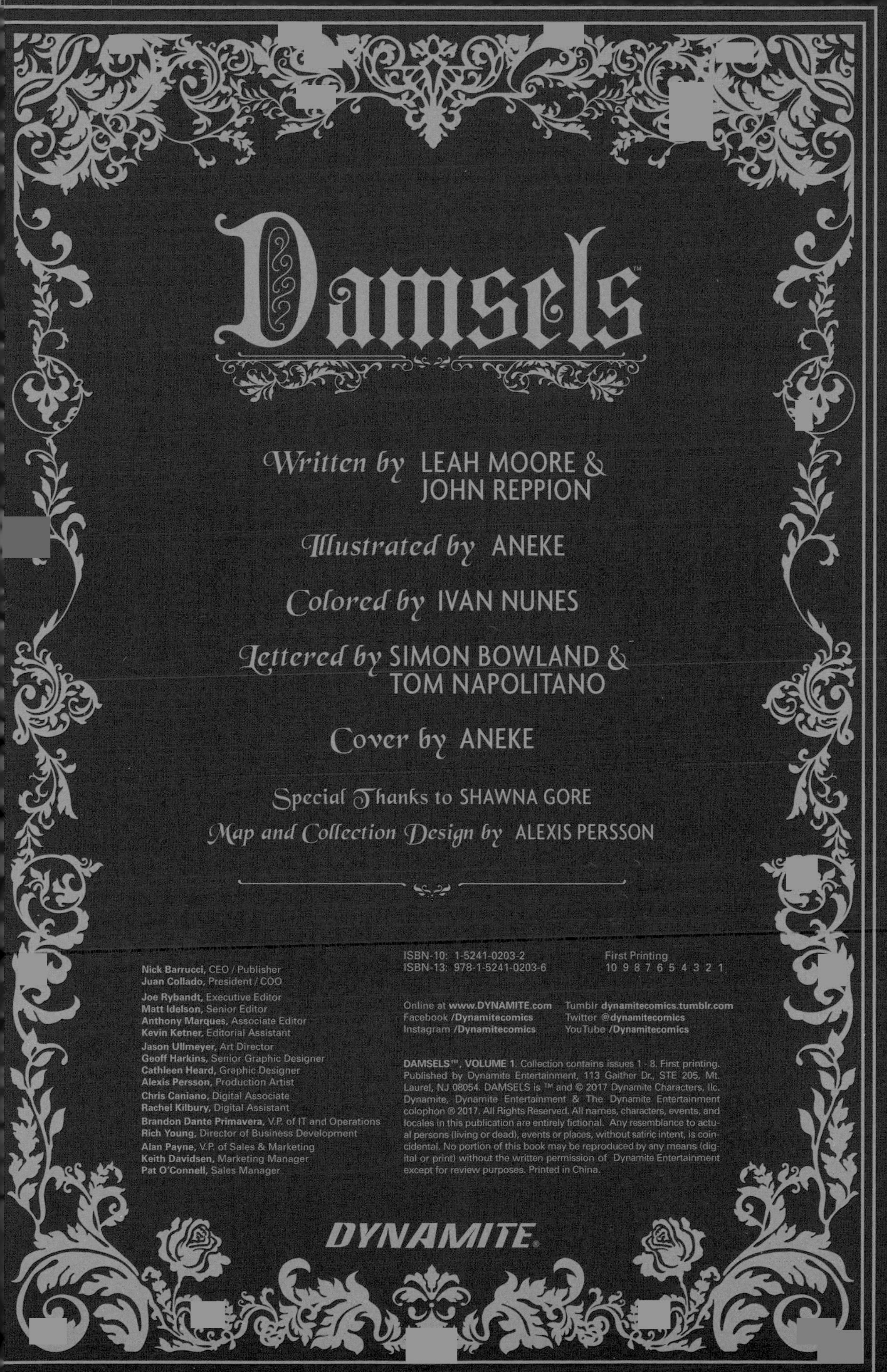

Damsels™

Written by LEAH MOORE & JOHN REPPION

Illustrated by ANEKE

Colored by IVAN NUNES

Lettered by SIMON BOWLAND & TOM NAPOLITANO

Cover by ANEKE

Special Thanks to SHAWNA GORE

Map and Collection Design by ALEXIS PERSSON

ISBN-10: 1-5241-0203-2
ISBN-13: 978-1-5241-0203-6

First Printing
10 9 8 7 6 5 4 3 2 1

Online at **www.DYNAMITE.com**
Facebook **/Dynamitecomics**
Instagram **/Dynamitecomics**
Tumblr **dynamitecomics.tumblr.com**
Twitter **@dynamitecomics**
YouTube **/Dynamitecomics**

DYNAMITE®

Chapter

Once upon a time...
COME QUICK!

OH HANS, I-I THINK IT MIGHT BE DEAD!

GLOMPSH
AARGH

MOTHER! MOTHER!
IT BIT ME!

MY GODS! WHAT'S HAPPENED?
THE FAIRY DID IT! LOOK, THERE IT GOES!
BAAH MEEAH
BAAH

...THAT'S ALL VERY WELL, MR. HITCHIN BUT WHAT ABOUT HER *FIRST BORN?* ANSWER ME THAT!
MADAM, I C'N ONLY REFER YOU TO OUR POLICY, WHICH I ASSUME YOU READ IN FULL *BEFORE* YOU PURCHASED THE CREATURE?
WHAT IN *BLAZES?*
OOPH!
WHUMP
OUTLANDER IDIOT! YOU ALMOST *KILLED* US!
WHAT D'YOU THINK YOU'RE PLAYIN' AT, EH?
MY STOCK!
EVERY LAST ONE OF THE BUGGERS!
CAN YOU 'EAR ME?
ARE YOU LISTENIN'?
I SAID, I 'OPE YOU'RE RICH, MISSUS! COS YOU OWE ME MORE'N A THOUSAND CROWNS!

YOU SEE YOU PAY HIM, MIND! HE OWES ME THIRTY FOR THE VICIOUS FIEND WHAT BIT OUR GRETA!
WHA-WHAT'S WRONG WITH YOU PEOPLE?
I'M NOT PAYING ANYONE *ANYTHING*. I DON'T HAVE ANY MONEY...
GET BACK HERE, YOU! SOMEONE FETCH THE WATCH!
...DIDN'T LAND ON THE *DWARVES* STALL YOU'LL NOTICE...
...DOESN'T LOOK ENTIRELY HUMAN *DOES* SHE? MIND YOU THESE OUTLANDERS HAVE THEIR OWN *WAYS*...
LOOKS LIKE A RUDDY TREE-DWELLER! WHAT'S IT DOING IN THE CITY?
MAKIN' TROUBLE! AND ON THE DAY O' THE ROYAL VISIT!
NO. THAT'S NOT... I'M *NOT*...
...WHY ARE THEY SAYING THAT?
WHAT...? WHAT AM I EVEN DOING HERE?

TALIA HAS OUTDONE HERSELF, MY DEAR. HER CAVALRY *GLEAMS* LIKE TREASURE.
EVEN THE KITCHEN WAGONS ARE IMMACULATE.
THAT'S TALIA FOR YOU-- *EVERYTHING* HAS TO BE PERFECT.
I-I CAN'T SAY I RECALL ACTUALLY *MEETING* THEIR HIGHNESSES BEFORE, DEAR...
OF COURSE YOU DO, DARLING, THEY CAME TO OUR WEDDING. WE WENT TO THEIRS.
HONESTLY, YOUR MEMORY IS GETTING WORSE. HAVE YOU BEEN TAKING YOUR INFUSIONS?
THIS COMPACT IS *INCREDIBLY* IMPORTANT, DEAR. WE NEED TO BE AT OUR VERY BEST FOR THIS VISIT!

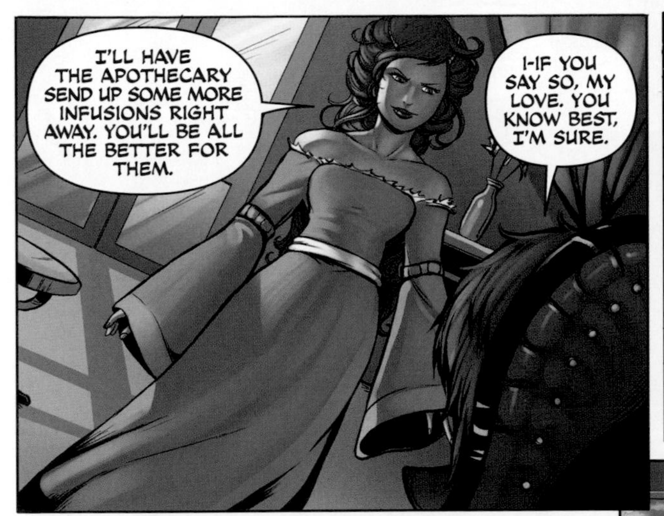
I'LL HAVE THE APOTHECARY SEND UP SOME MORE INFUSIONS RIGHT AWAY. YOU'LL BE ALL THE BETTER FOR THEM.
I-IF YOU SAY SO, MY LOVE. YOU KNOW BEST, I'M SURE.

I DON'T KNOW HOW YOU PUT UP WITH ME, REALLY I DON'T.
WHAT USE AM I TO YOU? I CAN'T SEE, I CAN'T *THINK!* YOU DESERVE BETTER, MY LOVE. *MUCH* BETTER.

PERSINE, I WON'T HAVE YOU SPEAK THAT WAY. WE WERE *MEANT* TO BE TOGETHER, *EVERYONE* KNOWS THAT.
COME ALONG. WE SHOULD BE IN THE ROBING CHAMBER BY NOW.
I BELIEVE KING AURORE IS BRINGING HIS FALCONS, SO PERHAPS YOU AND HE CAN GO OUT TOGETHER? ENJOY SOME SPORT?

I-I DO NOT KNOW HOW WELL I SHOULD MANAGE IT, MY LOVE, WITHOUT HAVING SIGHT OF THE BIRD...

AURORE WILL HELP YOU, I'M SURE. HE'S GOOD WITH ANIMALS.
IT'S THE GAUNTLET THEY RETURN TO, I THINK, NOT THE WEARER.
AH, SO YOU THINK I MIGHT BE ABLE TO HUNT THEN, AFTER ALL?

OH YES, DEAR. OF *COURSE.*
YOU'LL GET AN INSTINCT FOR YOUR PREY BEFORE LONG.
ALL HUNTERS DO.

ISN'T IT ROMANTIC?
WHAT IS?
I MEAN HE *RESCUED* HER, DIDN'T HE?
DID 'E?
YOU KNOW HE DID! RESCUED HER FROM... FROM...
'ANG ON, SHE WAS ASLEEP, WASN'T SHE?
THAT'S IT! ASLEEP!
FOR...FOR... A *HUNDRED YEARS*...? WAS IT?
LOVELY COUPLE, OF COURSE. LOVELY.
PERFECT, REALLY.
YET...SHE... SHE HARDLY LOOKS A DAY OVER *TWENTY.*
WE SHOULD TAKE THE LITTER MORE OFTEN, DON'T YOU THINK?

AND TRAVEL EVERYWHERE AT A SNAIL'S PACE?
HMM. I SUPPOSE IT IS RATHER SLOW.
IT'S PERFECT FOR BEING SEEN, BUT WE ARE NOT ALWAYS ON SHOW.

WAIT.
STOP.

STOP THAT WOMAN!

SORRY, CAN I JUST...CAN I JUST GET THROUGH PLEASE?
EXCUSE ME. I SAID, CAN I GET PAST YOU?

THERE SHE IS! WITH THE HAIR LIKE RED ROPE! YOU CAN'T MISS 'ER!

IN THE NAME OF QUEEN TALIA OF PERRAULT! STOP I SAY!
OH GODS! NOW WHAT?

I NEED TO GET OUT OF THIS KINGDOM!

MPHHH

THEIR ROYAL HIGHNESSES, QUEEN RAPUNZEL AND KING PERSINE!
LONG LIVE THE KING AND QUEEN!
IS...IS EVERYONE HERE?

YES, MY LOVE. ALL OF THEM.

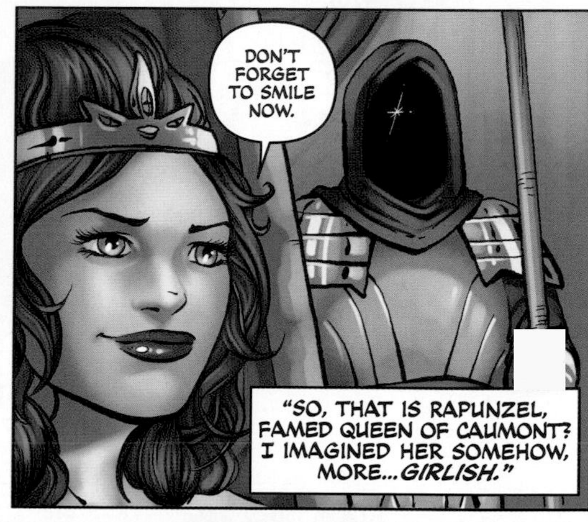
DON'T FORGET TO SMILE NOW.
"SO, THAT IS RAPUNZEL, FAMED QUEEN OF CAUMONT? I IMAGINED HER SOMEHOW, MORE...GIRLISH."

OBVIOUSLY HER MAJESTY TAKES HER POSITION VERY...SERIOUSLY, MUSTARDSEED. NOW, HOLD YOUR TONGUE.
HA! ASK THE WIND NOT TO BLOW WHY DON'T YOU!

THANK YOU, NAPAIOS, I AM QUITE AWARE OF THE FUTILITY OF MANY OF MY REQUESTS.
THE IMP IS BUT A WHELP, SIRE. HE WILL LEARN, IN TIME.
RATHER A WHELP, THAN THE PRODUCT OF SOME CAPRICIOUS GOAT HERD AND HIS PRIZE NANNY!

WHAT ARE YOU *THINKING?* WALKING ABOUT IN BROAD DAYLIGHT...

DON'T YOU REALIZE WHAT YOU'RE RISKING BY SHOWING YOURSELF?

I'LL WALK *WHERE* I WANT *WHEN* I WANT, AND I WON'T BE ASKING *YOU* FIRST!

OOPH!

PLEASE! YOU MUST UNDERSTAND THAT I WAS *NEVER* GOING TO HURT YOU! I NEVER...

I *UNDERSTAND* THAT PEOPLE WHO YANK ME INTO DARK ALLEYS CAN'T BE TRUSTED!

YOU FEEL IT, DON'T YOU? YOU FEEL *DIFFERENT* SOMEHOW? TO THE PEOPLE IN THE CROWD?
YOU HAVE... *MOMENTS*...WHERE YOU REMEMBER THINGS? FAMILIAR THINGS?
THESE IMAGES, DO YOU KNOW WHY YOU HAVE THEM ETCHED INTO YOUR FLESH?
I-I MUST HAVE JUST...*LIKED* THEM I SUPPOSE...I...I DON'T REALLY REMEMBER.
THINK. REALLY *THINK*. BACK TO WHEN YOU HAD THESE DONE, TO THE PAIN OF THE NEEDLE, THE INK BEING PUSHED INTO YOU.
I-I CAN REMEMBER...BITS. I CAN SMELL WOOD SMOKE, AND HEAR PEOPLE LAUGHING... DRUNK, I THINK.
"I *HAD* TO HAVE IT DONE, I *NEEDED* TO. I DON'T KNOW WHY NOW...WHY WOULD I DO THAT?"
"YOU *KNOW* WHY! YOU *KNOW!* DEEP INSIDE, YOU KNOW...*EVERYTHING!*"
B-BUT I DON'T UNDERSTAND...WHAT DOES ANY OF THIS MEAN? WHY ARE YOU SAYING ALL THIS?
BECAUSE... YOU AND I...
WE ARE *THE SAME!*

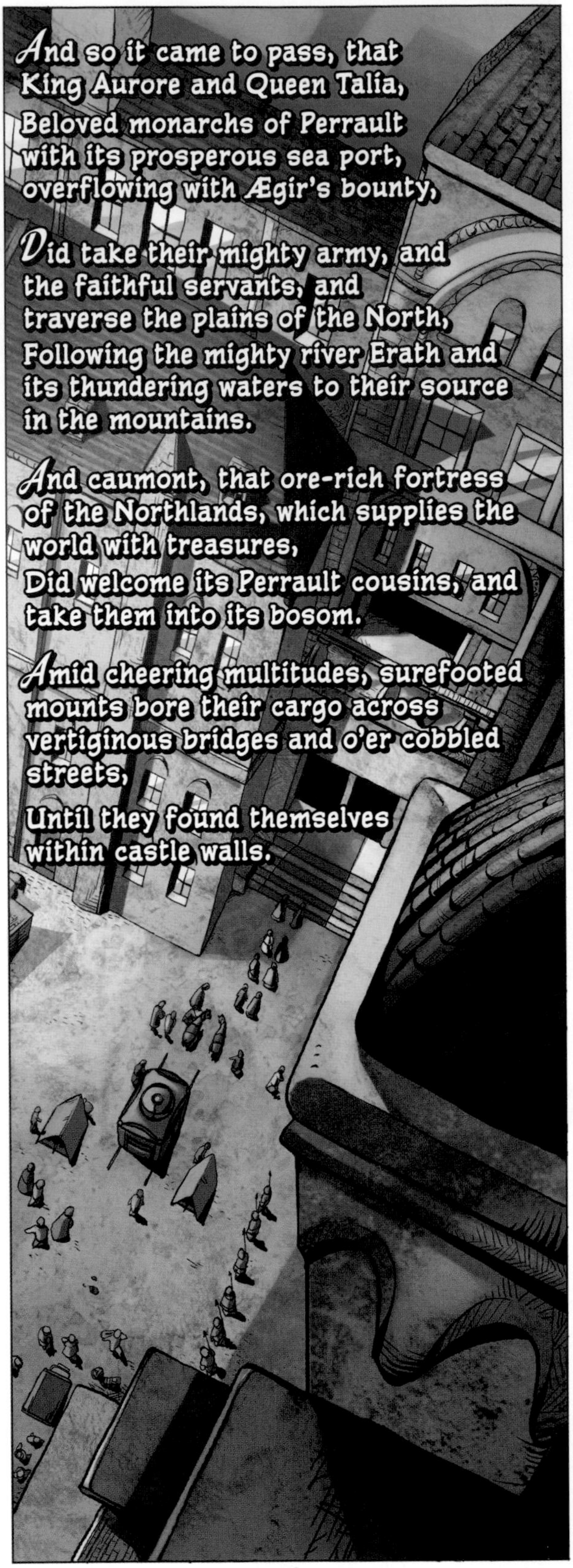

And so it came to pass, that King Aurore and Queen Talia,

Beloved monarchs of Perrault with its prosperous sea port, overflowing with Ægir's bounty,

Did take their mighty army, and the faithful servants, and traverse the plains of the North,

Following the mighty river Erath and its thundering waters to their source in the mountains.

And caumont, that ore-rich fortress of the Northlands, which supplies the world with treasures,

Did welcome its Perrault cousins, and take them into its bosom.

Amid cheering multitudes, surefooted mounts bore their cargo across vertiginous bridges and o'er cobbled streets,

Until they found themselves within castle walls.

King Aurore and his beautiful Queen were impressed at the splendor and richness which greeted them inside the castle,

Which proclaimed their hosts to be nobles of extraordinary wealth and superb taste.

Neither Queen Talia's own renowned beauty, nor the gleaming armor of her men at arms,

Could outshine the beauty of the castle that day.

Wonder heaped on wonder as they drew closer to the throne room of their hosts,

Until it seemed no thing of greater beauty could exist.

Queen Talia, King Aurore and their men paused before those great oaken doors

Shaking the shining marvels from their minds eye, and preparing themselves for their reception, by glorious Caumont, and its King and Queen.

If the nobles of Caumont had grown used to marvels and beauty, then they did not show it that day.

No man nor woman could turn their gaze from the spectacle of Perrault's most beloved son and daughter.

Gasps rippled across the room, to see Talia take her husband's arm, and walk so tall along the aisle.

Many saw their own awed faces reflected in the armour of that glorious phalanx.

I ALMOST BELIEVED... I ALMOST FELL FOR THE WHOLE THING! THE WHOLE *RIDICULOUS*...
WHY AM I TALKING TO YOU? WHY AM I WASTING MY RUDDY BREATH?
IT'S TRUE... *IT IS!* YOUR TATTOOS TELL A TALE!
EXACTLY! A TALE! SINCE WHEN WAS A STORY *REASON* ENOUGH TO GO YANKING PEOPLE OFF THE STREET?
I'VE GOT NEWS FOR YOU, SHORTY. *STORIES AREN'T REAL!*
DO YOU EVEN *KNOW* WHAT I'VE BEEN THROUGH TODA--
STOP WHERE YOU ARE!
STOP IN THE NAME OF QUEEN *TALIA!*
COME ON! THIS WAY!
PLEASE GODS, NOT AGAIN.

YOU LOOK RADIANT AS *EVER* RAPUNZEL!
NEXT TO *YOU* I FEEL VERY PLAIN.
I'M IMPRESSED WITH CAUMONT CASTLE, COUSIN KING.
IT HAS BEEN MANY YEARS SINCE I SAW IT. RAPUNZEL TELLS ME IT HASN'T CHANGED.

ALL IS NOT WELL. THERE ARE *ENEMIES* AMONG US.

FELLOW MONARCHS, LOYAL SUBJECTS AND TRUSTED FRIENDS, IT GIVES ME ENORMOUS PLEASURE TO RECEIVE YOU AS MY GUESTS.
CAUMONT AND PERRAULT HAVE BEEN PARTNERS IN TRADE, EVER SINCE A ROUTE COULD BE TRACED ACROSS THE NORTHERN PLAINS.

THEY'RE STILL RIGHT BEHIND US!

I HOPE YOU'VE GOT A PLAN! AS IN, A GOOD SOLID "WON'T GET US KILLED" TYPE OF PLAN.

RIGHT NOW, I DON'T HAVE A CHOICE, BUT LATER ON WE'LL HAVE TO SIT AND GO THROUGH WAYS TO EARN TRUST, AND WAYS NOT TO.

THEY'RE GETTING TIRED. I THINK WE'RE GOING TO LOSE THEM!

HA! I THINK YOU'RE RIGHT! WON'T CATCH US NOW!
WOAH!

WE MIGHT NEED A RETHINK.

WHAT'S HAPPENING?
A SPY!
AN ASSASSIN!

NOT SO FAST!

MAGIC!
≠GASP≠
GODS HELP US, IT'S MAGIC!

STOP THAT THING! THAT'S AN ORDER!

WHAT'S HAPPENING? WHERE IS IT?
IT'S COMING BACK!

WHAT?!
COME ON.
NO! STOP!
AARGH
SPLSH
SPLSH

IT'S MAGIC! MAGIC!
DON'T LOOK AT IT! DON'T LOOK!
IT'LL TURN US ALL INTO SOMETHING!
IS IT ENCHANTING US? AM I BEING ENCHANTED?

WATCH OUT!
SOMEONE DO SOMETHING!

SPLAT

IT'S ALL RIGHT. EVERYTHING'S ALL RIGHT.

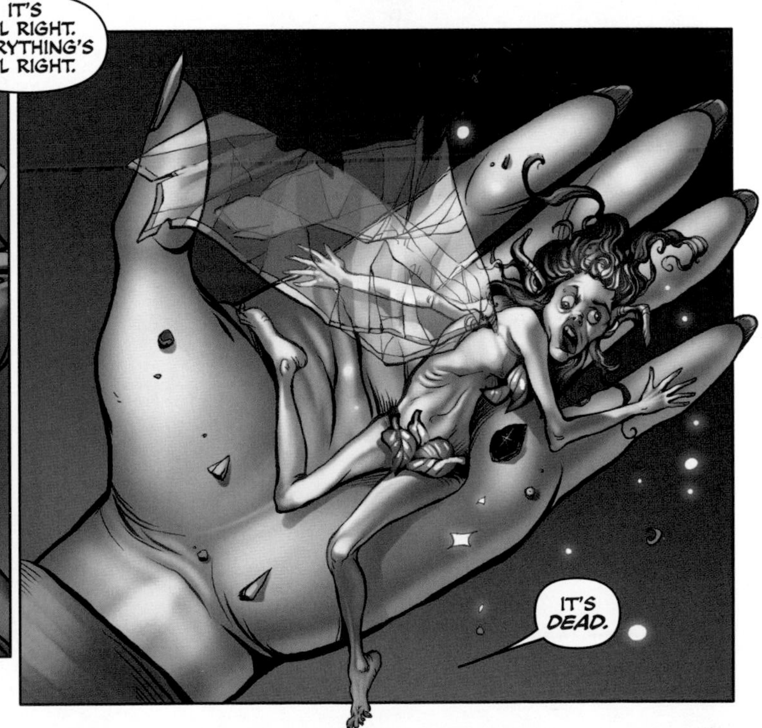
IT'S DEAD.

Chapter
2

A long, long time ago, a priest desired a church be built atop a hill.
Digging down, his men awoke a dormant Wyrmling.
Unbeknownst to priest and flock alike, this Wyrmling nested beneath the churchyard.
The beast consumed all who were buried, growing larger and larger.
All too soon, the adult Wyrm was bold enough to venture from its lair.
Coiling around the hill, it devoured anything within reach.
One day the priest heard of a cockered laying a egg.
Nesting the egg in straw, he set a toad to hatching it.
For tho he know a cock's egg warmed by a toad will hatch into a Cockatrice.
And such a beast has certain powers.
No sooner had the Cockatrice emerged than it was caught up in a sack.
And this sack was taken to the Wyrm's lair.
When the bag was thrown open, the Wyrm struck hungrily.
And meeting the Cockatrice's magical gaze, the Wyrm was turned to stone.
The priest, overcome with joy at the monster's defeat, forgot the danger before him.
And rushing forward, he too was transformed to stone.
The Cockatrice was destroyed by turning its gaze upon itself and shattering its remains.
The servants returned their stone priest to his church...

AREN'T THEY YOUR... COUSINS, OR SOMETHING?

OR AM I MISUNDERSTANDING THE WHOLE *TAIL* SITUATION?

I'M NOT A FISH.

BUT MOST THINGS IN THE SEA DO EAT FISH. INCLUDING MANY OTHER FISH.

THE SEA? SO, YOU'RE PRETTY FAR FROM HOME THEN?

IS THAT WHY THEY WERE AFTER YOU? BACK IN CAUMONT, I MEAN?
BECAUSE OF...OF WHAT YOU ARE?
THOSE GUARDS WERE MORE INTERESTED IN YOU THAN ME.

BUT YES, QUEEN TALIA'S PERSONAL GUARD WILL HAVE HAD SPECIAL ORDERS FOR WHAT TO DO WITH US, AND PEOPLE LIKE US.

WHAT DO YOU MEAN "PEOPLE LIKE US"?
WE'RE BOTH IN TROUBLE, YES, BUT THAT'S NOT WHAT I MEANT.
I MEAN WE AREN'T LIKE OTHER PEOPLE.

I MEAN, WELL...YOU'RE A MERMAID AREN'T YOU?

"I-IT'S NOT AS SIMPLE AS THAT.
"I MEAN, WHEN I WAS YOUNGER, I WAS A MERMAID THEN...

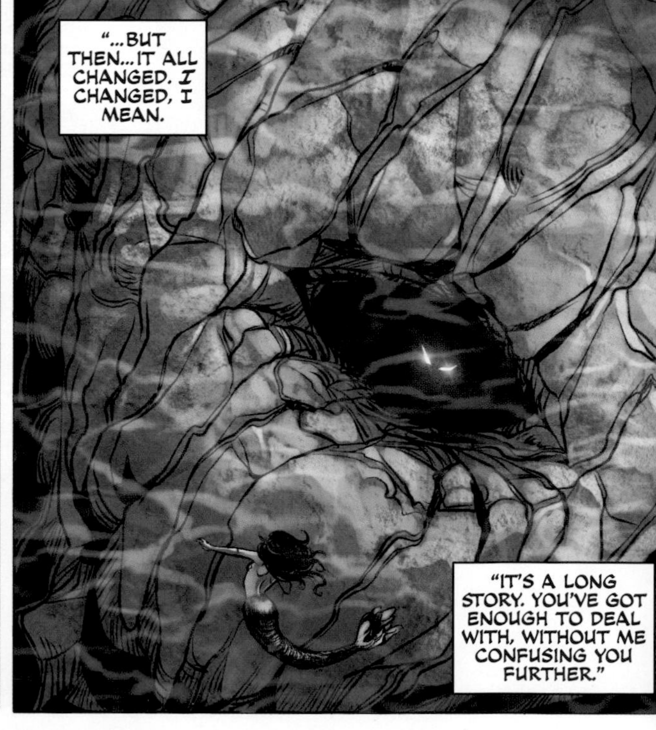
"...BUT THEN...IT ALL CHANGED. I CHANGED, I MEAN.
"IT'S A LONG STORY. YOU'VE GOT ENOUGH TO DEAL WITH, WITHOUT ME CONFUSING YOU FURTHER."

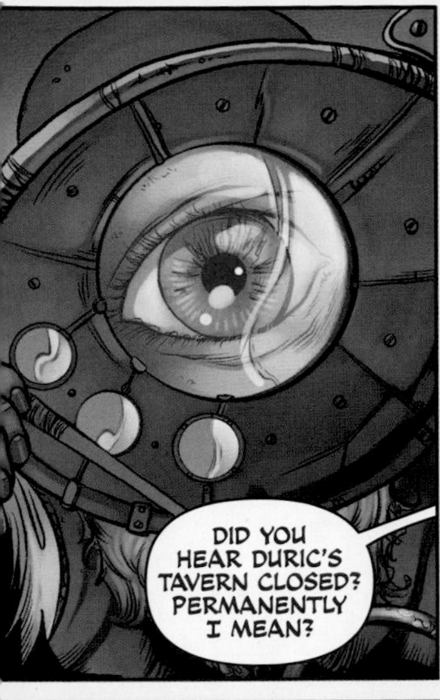
DID YOU HEAR DURIC'S TAVERN CLOSED? PERMANENTLY I MEAN?

REALLY? GONE? BUT DURIC'S HAS BEEN THERE FOR YEARS!
SEEMS SO. IT'S ALL BOARDED UP, AND NOBODY'S SEEN HIM.

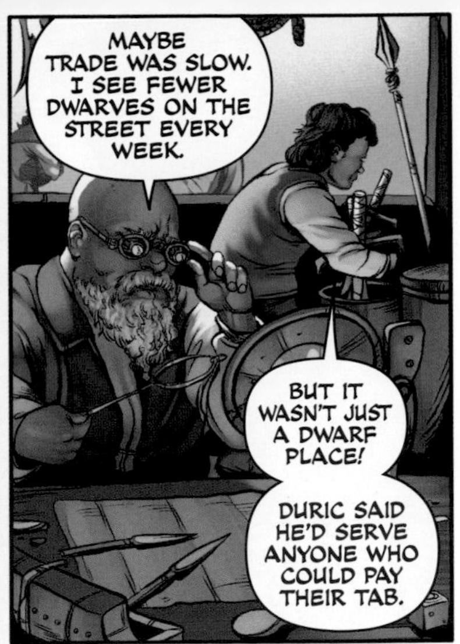
MAYBE TRADE WAS SLOW. I SEE FEWER DWARVES ON THE STREET EVERY WEEK.
BUT IT WASN'T JUST A DWARF PLACE!
DURIC SAID HE'D SERVE ANYONE WHO COULD PAY THEIR TAB.

MAYBE FOLK WON'T MIX WITH *FAE* NO MORE, *GNOMES* AND SUCH.
MAYBE. I NEVER MET A GNOME COULD HOLD ITS ALE.
GODS, ITS SLOW TODAY.

I WAS THINKING IF YOU WON'T MISS ME, I'LL HEAD OVER TO SEE WHAT THIS PROCLAMATION'S ALL ABOUT?
I WANTED TO HEAR THAT AN' ALL.
I'LL COME OVER WITH YOU. KEEP YOU COMPANY.

AYE, IT'S NOT 'TILL TWO, SO WE'LL GO ONCE YOU'VE DONE THE LUNCH RUSH. WISH THEY'D BLOOMIN' RUSH US...

DO YOU KNOW WHAT THIS IS ALL ABOUT THEN?
NEW STOCK ARRIVING SOON
THERE WAS SOME KIND OF ATTACK LAST NIGHT AT THE PALACE.
A THIEF, OR AN ASSASSIN, OR SOMETHING. MAYBE THEY CAUGHT HIM?

THEY'D BE FOOLS TO TRY IT DURING THE ROYAL VISIT THOUGH, WOULDN'T THEY?
DID YOU SEE QUEEN TALIA'S GUARDS YESTERDAY IN THE PARADE? THEY LOOKED LETHAL!
I WOULDN'T SAY LETHAL... *SHINY*, CERTAINLY!
THAT'S FIGHTING TALK!
RECKON YOU COULD TAKE THEM, DO YOU? THE LEGENDARY BRÖKK AGAINST TALIA'S ELITE COTERIE?

I WOULDN'T GO THAT FAR. I'D SCUFF THEIR BREASTPLATES, SO THEY RAN OFF TO POLISH 'EM UP AGAIN!
OR PART THEIR HAIR ON THE WRONG SIDE, IF I WAS FEELING NASTY.

THERE YOU GO AGAIN! I'VE *"GOT ENOUGH TO DEAL WITH"*?
WHAT'S THAT SUPPOSED TO MEAN?

HOW DID YOU GET TO CAUMONT? WHAT WERE YOU DOING THERE?
YOU CAN'T REMEMBER, CAN YOU? YOU MUSTN'T, OR ELSE YOU WOULDN'T HAVE LET YOURSELF BE SEEN!
LOOK, YES... I MEAN NO, BUT... I-I HAVE A LOT OF TROUBLE WITH MY MEMORY.

I... I THINK I WAS TRYING TO GET TO CAUMONT FOR A LONG TIME. YEARS MAYBE...?
I MUST HAVE HAD A REASON, BUT... WELL, LIKE I SAID, I FORGET THINGS...
RAPA, LOOK AT YOUR ARMS. WHAT DO YOU SEE THERE?

THE TOWER, THE FLOWERS. RAPUNZEL STUFF. SO WHAT? IT'S JUST A STORY.
SO, TELL ME THE STORY THEN. HOW DOES IT GO?

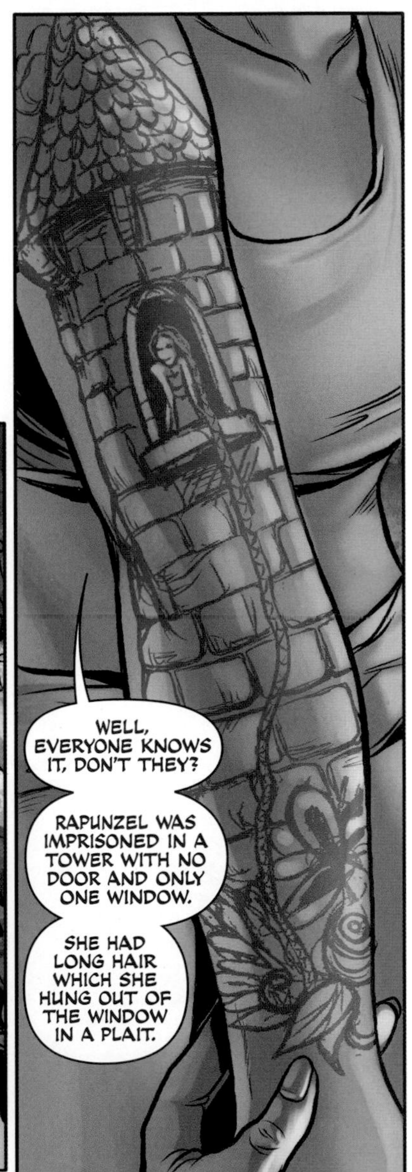
WELL, EVERYONE KNOWS IT, DON'T THEY?
RAPUNZEL WAS IMPRISONED IN A TOWER WITH NO DOOR AND ONLY ONE WINDOW.
SHE HAD LONG HAIR WHICH SHE HUNG OUT OF THE WINDOW IN A PLAIT.

"A HANDSOME PRINCE CLIMBED UP HER HAIR...
"...AND THEY FELL IN LOVE...OR...OR WAS IT NOT THAT?

"DID HE FALL? DID HE FALL FROM THE TOWER INSTEAD?"

AND THEN... THEN...
WHO DID IT? WHO LOCKED HER IN THE TOWER?

I CAN'T REMEMBER, ALL RIGHT? NOT EVEN A SIMPLE STORY, A CHILDREN'S TALE...
YOU CAN! LOOK HERE! SEE FOR YOURSELF!

IT--IT'S A WITCH, ISN'T IT? A WITCH TRICKED THEM BOTH.
GO ON! WHO IS SHE? THE WITCH? WHAT'S HER NAME?

"SHE'S JUST A WITCH! YOU KNOW, THE WICKED WITCH, THE EVIL OLD WITCH... MOTHER...MOTHER SOMETHING.
"MOTHER GOTHEL? IS THAT IT?"

MOTHER GOTHEL! THE WITCH!
SO, WHO DID THIS TO YOU? WHO MADE YOU FORGET?

ARE YOU SURE YOU WON'T JOIN US, RAPUNZEL MY DEAR?
OH, I THINK THE TWO MIGHTY KINGS, UNITED IN THEIR CAUSE, SENDS OUT MUCH MORE POWERFUL MESSAGE.
BESIDES, QUEEN TALIA AND I HAVE MUCH TO DISCUSS.
AS YOU WISH, MY LOVE. I SHALL DO MY BEST.
LOYAL SUBJECTS, IT IS WITH DEEPEST SORROW AND REGRET THAT I ADDRESS YOU ALL TODAY. I BRING ILL NEWS.
PEACEFUL CAUMONT HAS BEEN ATTACKED BY AN ENEMY. AN ENEMY WHICH NESTLED IN OUR VERY BOSOM.
"MANY OF YOU WILL HAVE HEARD, THAT AGENTS OF THIS ENEMY ATTACKED YOUR KING AND QUEEN, AND THEIR ROYAL GUESTS LAST NIGHT.
"THIS ATTACK WAS WITNESSED BY THE ENTIRE COURT, SO BRAZEN WAS ITS NATURE.
"I CALL ON YOU NOW FOR HELP IN ROOTING OUT THIS ENEMY WHEREVER YOU FIND THEM. WHATEVER GUISE THEY MAY TAKE.
LET NO MAN BE *ABOVE* SUSPICION, NOR *IMMUNE* TO THE PROCESS OF THE LAW.
"THIS ENEMY USED *MAGIC* TO ATTACK CAUMONT, BUT IT IS THIS VERY THING WHICH SHALL BE THEIR DOWNFALL.
"WHEREVER OUR ENEMY HIDES, THERE WILL BE MAGIC. THEREFORE, WHEREVER THERE IS MAGIC, WE SHALL FIND OUR ENEMY."

OUR WAYS ARE NOT THEIRS, THEY *BETRAY* THEMSELVES WITH TRAITS THEY CANNOT DISGUISE. ALL YOU NEED DO IS REMAIN VIGILANT.
ONLY BY DOING THIS, WILL WE BE SAFE, ONLY THIS WAY, WILL CAUMONT BE *VICTORIOUS!*
"IT IS THE *DUTY* OF EVERY MAN, WOMAN, AND CHILD TO HUNT DOWN THE ENEMY, HUNT DOWN THOSE PURVEYORS OF SORCERY, AND GIVE THEM OVER TO JUSTICE!
"LOYAL SUBJECTS DO YOUR DUTY! FOR CAUMONT! FOR FREEDOM!"
LET THESE WORDS BE YOUR MANTRA, LET THEM GUIDE YOU EVERY DAY:
EXPEL ALL ENEMIES FROM THIS KINGDOM. LET NOTHING THRIVE THAT MAGIC BE!
EXPEL ALL ENEMIES FROM THIS KINGDOM. LET NOTHING THRIVE THAT MAGIC BE!
EXPEL ALL ENEMIES FROM THIS KINGDOM. LET NOTHING THRIVE THAT MAGIC BE!
"EXPEL ALL ENEMIES FROM THIS KINGDOM. LET NOTHING THRIVE THAT MAGIC BE!"
EXPEL ALL ENEMIES FROM THIS KINGDOM. LET NOTHING THRIVE THAT MAGIC BE!
EXPEL ALL ENEMIES FROM THIS KINGDOM. LET NOTHING THRIVE THAT MAGIC BE!
EXPEL ALL ENEMIES FROM THIS KINGDOM. LET NOTHING THRIVE THAT MAGIC BE!

SO, YOU THINK THAT THE WITCH--THE ACTUAL WITCH--WHO IMPRISONED RAPUNZEL, CAST A SPELL TO MAKE ME FORGET THE STORY OF RAPUNZEL?
ARE YOU SAYING YOU DON'T BELIEVE IN WITCHES?
IT'S NOT ABOUT BELIEF!
IT'S ABOUT WHETHER IT MAKES ANY SENSE!

LOOK, MAYBE I...
I SUPPOSE I MUST BE OBSESSED WITH RAPUNZEL... PERHAPS I JUST WANTED TO MEET HER?

THE TATTOOS ARE TO REMIND YOU WHO YOU REALLY ARE.
WHEN THE MEMORIES CAME BACK, OR CLICKED INTO PLACE, YOU MUST HAVE RUSHED TO HAVE SOMETHING PERMANENT BEFORE YOU FORGOT.
WHO I AM? WHAT DO YOU MEAN?

I'M NOBODY! I DON'T BELIEVE ANY OF THIS! ABOUT RAPUNZEL OR MOTHER GOTHEL!
I'M ENCHANTED? BEWITCHED?
WHAT FOR?

BECAUSE YOU'RE THE REAL RAPUNZEL.

RMMMBBBLLLLLLL

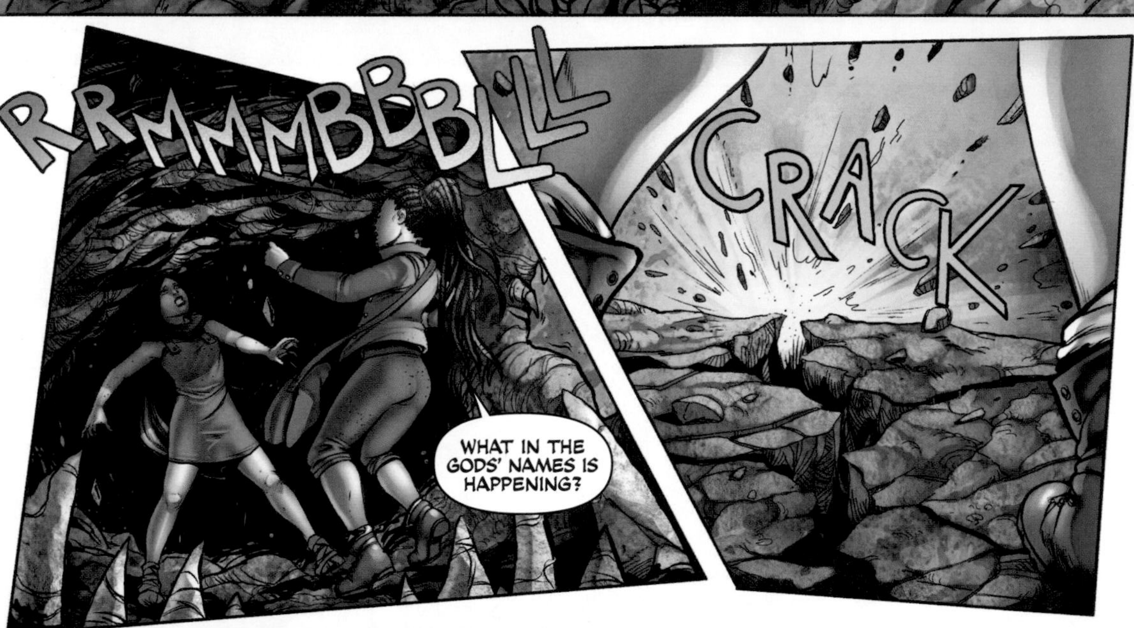
RRMMMBBBLLL
WHAT IN THE GODS' NAMES IS HAPPENING?
CRACK

LOOK OUT!

EXPEL ALL ENEMIES FROM THIS KINGDOM. LET NOTHING THRIVE THAT MAGIC BE!
ULF?
AM I MISSING SOMETHING?

WHAT ARE YOU DOING HERE, *DWARF?*

I CAME WITH YOU, YOU *MUTTONHEAD.*
IS THIS SUPPOSED TO BE SOME SORT OF JOKE?

HERE IN CAUMONT, I MEAN. IN *OUR* KINGDOM.
YOU DON'T BELONG HERE.
MY FAMILY'S BEEN IN CAUMONT FOR THREE-HUNDRED YEARS. YOUR MOTHER'S FROM *PERRAULT!*

BUT YOU STILL *SNEAK* OFF BACK TO THE MOUNTAINS NOW AND AGAIN. YOU *ALL* DO.
NONE OF *US* KNOWS WHAT *YOU* GET UP TO UP THERE.

WHO--OR *WHAT*--YOU'RE MEETING WITH, PRAYING TO, TAKING *ORDERS* FROM.

KRAK
OOPH
I DON'T KNOW WHAT IN THE GODS' NAMES IS SUPPOSED TO BE GOING ON HERE, BUT I'VE HAD ENOUGH.
WE AIN'T FINISHED WITH YOU YET, CAVE BOY.
IS THAT RIGHT?
EXPEL ALL ENEMIES FROM THIS KINGDOM. LET NOTHING THRIVE THAT MAGIC BE!
AYE, I HEARD YOU THE FIRST TIME.
COME ON THEN.
WHO'S NEXT?

TAKE MY HAND!

OH...!
SKREEEE

WHUMP
UNGH
BOUMPH
RRMMMBBBLLL
RAPA? RAPA!
CAN YOU HEAR ME?

...TRULY STIRRING, YOUR MAJESTY. JUST THE KIND OF THING YOUR SUBJECTS NEEDED TO HEAR!
EVERY ABLE BODIED MAN WILL BE EAGER TO VOLUNTEER FOR OUR CAUSE NOW!

CAUSE?
AH, YOUR MAJESTY, FORGIVE ME. I WAS REFERRING SPECIFICALLY TO THE KING'S ARMY.
BUT, OF COURSE, I MEANT THE COMPACT BETWEEN OUR CAUMONT, YOUR OWN KINGDOM OF PERRAULT, AND SOON THAT OF VILLENEUVE.

YES NATURALLY, WE... NEED A STRONG MILITARY...DON'T WE?
AND YOUR ARMY IS HERE ALREADY OF COURSE, BROTHER-AURORE.

INDEED IT IS, BROTHER PERSINE. THE MIGHTIEST ARMY EVER RAISED BY PERRAULT.
JUST IMAGINE THEIR *COMBINED* STRENGTH, YOUR HIGHNESSES. UNPARALLELED. *UNSTOPPABLE!*
I THANK THE GODS--THE *TRUE* GODS, NATURALLY--THAT I SHOULD LIVE IN SUCH WONDROUS TIMES, YOUR MAJESTIES.

KING PERSINE DID A MAGNIFICENT JOB. HE HAS A GREAT GIFT WITH PUBLIC SPEAKING.
OH, I *AM* PLEASED EVERYTHING WENT WELL!

AND I.
YOU ALWAYS WERE SO GOOD AT DELIVERING OUR MESSAGE TO THE SUBJECTS, MY KING.

WELL, IT JUST SORT OF *COMES* TO ME...
INDEED? WELL THERE IS MUCH TO BE DISCUSSED IN PREPARATION FOR OUR JOURNEY EASTWARD.
LETS HOPE YOU ARE SIMILARLY *INSPIRED.*

WELL...PERSINE'S ADVISOR FELT CERTAIN THE SPEECH WOULD INSPIRE MANY TO ENLIST IN YOUR ARMY, DID HE NOT, COUSIN KING?
OH CERTAINLY, YES.
OUR *TWO* MIGHTY ARMIES, MARCHING TOGETHER TO VILLENEUVE, EH?

AND JUST IMAGINE HOW POWERFUL WE *THREE* SHALL BE TOGETHER.

The Kingdom of Villeneuve.

ARE YOU AWAKE, MY LOVE?

I HAVE BROUGHT FOOD FOR YOU.

ROAR

W-WHAT HAPPENED?
YOU HIT YOUR HEAD.
WAIT, THIS...THIS IS THE CHURCH. WHAT ARE WE DOING UP HERE?
STONE FLOOR!
YOU THINK THAT'LL MAKE A DIFFERENCE?
I HOPE SO.
BUT PERHAPS NOT.

KRRAASH

The great Wyrm was not dead, however, merely frozen—spellbound in a prison of stone.
There it remained, coiled around Wyrm Hill for hundreds of years, until one day a powerful magic broke the Cockatrice curse.
And so, waked from its centuried slumber, the Wyrm turned its anger upon the church of the man who had bested it.
During this onslaught, a certain figure was smashed into a hundred pieces.
The creature lacked the intelligence to know the significance of that act of destruction.
Its appetite for destruction sated, the Wyrm burrowed down through fathoms of soil, returning to the bowels of the world without ever understanding.
For the figure was no statue after all, it was the petrified body of that self same priest.
But his curse had never been broken.

Chapter

THERE WAS ONCE A KING WITH TWELVE DAUGHTERS, EACH MORE BEAUTIFUL THAN THE LAST.
THE PRINCESSES ALL SLEPT TOGETHER IN ONE ROOM AND WHEN THEY WENT TO BED, THEIR DOOR WAS LOCKED BY THE KING HIMSELF.
YET EVERY SINGLE MORNING, WHEN THE DOOR WAS UNBOLTED, A PAIR OF EACH DAUGHTER'S FINEST DANCING SHOES WAS FOUND TO BE QUITE WORN THROUGH.
AND THIS VEXED THE KING GREATLY.
WHAT THE KING NEVER KNEW WAS THAT EACH NIGHT, AFTER HE TURNED HIS KEY, HIS ELDEST DAUGHTER WOULD GIVE A SECRET KNOCK.
AT THAT KNOCK, THE PRINCESS'S BED WOULD SINK INTO THE FLOOR TO REVEAL A GREAT STAIRCASE HIDDEN BENEATH.
AND, WEARING THEIR FINEST DANCING SHOES, THE TWELVE SISTERS WOULD DESCEND TOGETHER.
"DOWN AND DOWN THEY WENT UNTIL AT LAST THEY CAME TO AN UNDERGROUND LAKE.
"AND AT THE SIDE OF THE LAKE, TWELVE FAIRY PRINCES WAITED FOR THEM IN TWELVE BOATS.
"ON THE OTHER SIDE OF THE LAKE STOOD A FINE ILLUMINATED CASTLE, FROM WHICH CAME MERRY MUSIC.
"MERRY MUSIC MADE FOR DANCING."

His deep Dark eyes
Keep watch on his kingdom
And the mystery
that sleep safe inside
His hall Its towers of stone
Shall not be overthrown
For eternity
It is guarded by the king
Insanity and the power
that it brings
Madness reigns
In the Hall of the
Mountain King
TKTKKTKTK
KRASH

SKREEE
KRUNNNP
IS THERE ANYBODY THERE? ANYBODY?
EXTRAORDINARY...
HOW VERY UNPLEASANT!
HA-HA, I'M ALIVE!
ALIVE!

And so it was that a small band of Caumont dwarves took up arms.

Centuries earlier, their ancestors had descended from the mountains to lend their strength in the founding of the kingdom.

Never would those mountain-folk have imagined that their kind might one day be persecuted within the very walls their axes hewed from the ancient stone.

And never would they have tolerated such.

THE MERRY INN
THE QUIET INN
What dwarves saw as justified retaliation for violence wrought against their brother, the humans saw as clear evidence of their hatred of man.

The oldest of friends, the most trusted of neighbours, all became sworn enemies in a matter of moments.

And the streets of Caumont were transformed into a battleground.

YOUR, MAJESTIES?
MY APOLOGIES, BUT...IF I MIGHT INTRUDE, YOUR MAJESTIES?
COME! ENTER! JOIN US MY GOOD FELLOW!
HAVE YOU EVER SEEN SUCH GRACE? SUCH BEAUTY? COME AND SIT WITH US!
I--AH. I THANK YOU YOUR MAJESTY, YOU ARE MORE THAN KIND, BUT I CAME SEEKING KING PERSINE'S EAR FOR A MOMENT.
WHAT NEWS? IS SOMETHING AMISS?
MY KING, IT'S THE DWARVES.
AFTER YOUR SPEECH, THERE WAS A REBELLION. AN UPRISING, IF YOU WILL.
AN UPRISING? NEVER.
I CANNOT BELIEVE IT OF OUR DWARVES. THEY HAVE NEVER REBELLED IN THE HISTORY OF CAUMONT.
I... I CAN SHOW YOU, SIRE, BUT WHAT ABOUT YOUR QUEEN?
THE LADY RAPUNZEL ENTERTAINS HER GUEST, QUEEN TALIA, THIS EVENING...

"...AND DOES NOT WISH TO BE DISTURBED."
I CAN'T BELIEVE YOUR IDIOT GUARDS LET HER GET AWAY! HOW MUCH ARE YOU PAYING THEM? SHE SHOULD BE *DEAD!*
SHE *IS* DEAD.

THE FALL INTO THE WATER MAY WELL HAVE BEEN ENOUGH TO KILL HER.
BUT, IF SHE DID LIVE, THE NEW SPELL WILL FINISH HER OFF.

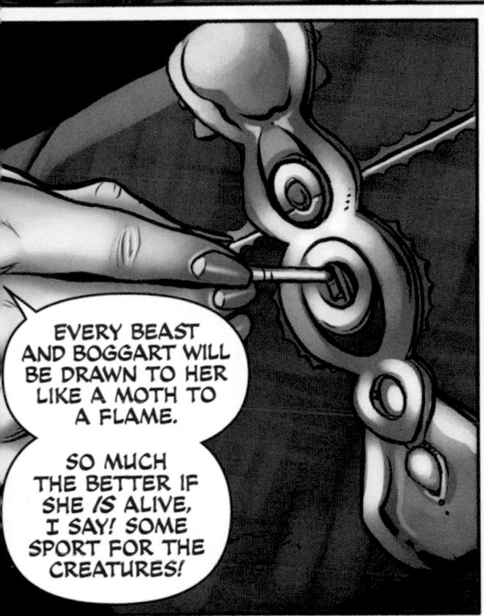
EVERY BEAST AND BOGGART WILL BE DRAWN TO HER LIKE A MOTH TO A FLAME.
SO MUCH THE BETTER IF SHE *IS* ALIVE, I SAY! SOME SPORT FOR THE CREATURES!

YOU LET YOUR GLEE CLOUD YOUR MIND, MY DEAR. IT IS ALWAYS BETTER TO TIE UP LOOSE ENDS WHEREVER POSSIBLE.
YOU HAVE NOTHING TO FEAR! THE SPELL IS CAST, AND THE KINGDOM'S ENCHANTMENT IS TWICE AS STRONG NOW THAT WE ARE TOGETHER!

"WHAT OF THE OTHER GIRL YOUR GUARDS SAW?
"SHE COULD BE ONE OF THE OTHERS!"

"OH MY DEAR, YOU WORRY TOO MUCH.
"SHE WAS NOBODY! WE'D HAVE SENSED IT, OTHERWISE. BESIDES, IF THEY WERE TOGETHER, SHE WILL BE DEAD TOO."

FETCH WINE FOR OUR GUEST! AT ONCE!
WHERE IS THIS PLACE? WHO ARE YOU?
IT IS CURIOUSLY ATTIRED, BUT I THINK NONETHELESS IT IS A HUMAN!
I AM HUMAN, YES...SO WHAT DOES THAT MAKE YOU? APART FROM INTRUSIVE I MEAN?
IT HAS HORRIBLE STICK HAIR, BUT ITS FACE IS NOT *TOO* UGLY!
MUSIC! PLEASE, FOR OUR LOVELY GUEST.
THIS REALLY ISN'T...THAT IS, I DON'T WANT YOU TO...
NO, REALLY I HAVE GOT TO GO, I HAVE TO FIND MY FRIEND. I HAVE TO LEAVE!
I REALLY DON'T HAVE TIME TO--
--DANCE.
RELAX, MY LOVELY! ENJOY YOURSELF, THE DANCE IS JUST BEGINNING!
THERE ARE *SO MANY* DANCES TO BE DANCED BEFORE DAWN!

DAWN? I DON'T HAVE TIME TO SPEND ALL NIGHT DANCING WITH YOU!
NONSENSE MY LOVELY, WE HAVE ALL THE TIME IN THE WORLD, JUST LISTEN TO THE MUSIC, AND LET YOURSELF...GO...
THAT'S IT! YOU FEEL IT DON'T YOU?
INSIDE OF YOU...THE MUSIC LIFTS YOUR FEET AND MAKES YOU LIGHTER THAN AIR!
I-I FEEL... SOMETHING... YES.
IT FEELS SO NATURAL DOESN'T IT?
YOU AND I, MOVING LIKE THIS, WITH THE MUSIC, MOVING *TOGETHER*...
IT *DOES*...IT REALLY DOES...HOW EASY IT IS! AS IF MY FEET KNOW THE STEPS!
HOW IS IT THAT I CAN DANCE WITH YOU ALL, AND NOT HEAR THE MUSIC STOP? I DON'T REMEMBER CHANGING PARTNERS!
BECAUSE YOU ARE ENJOYING YOURSELF, YOU BECOME LOST IN THE MUSIC! ENJOY IT MY DEAR, ENJOY THIS NIGHT OF PLEASURE...
MY GODS! I *AM* LOST! I ALMOST BELIEVED IT ALL TOO!
THIS IS ALL A SHAM! A HORRIBLE TRICK!
CALM YOURSELF MY DEAR, IT WAS NOT INTENDED TO SCARE YOU, ONLY AMUSE!
AND YOU HAVE BEEN AMUSED, HAVE YOU NOT?

Villeneuve.
"HANDS REACH OUT ACROSS TIME AND SPACE, SISTERS. DO YOU HEAR MY CALL? DO YOU RESPOND?"
"AYE, WE RESPOND. OUR HANDS REACH ALSO. WE FORGE THIS LINK THAT IT MAY NOT BE TORN ASUNDER."
HOW ARE YOU, MY SISTERS? WAS YOUR MEETING A JOYOUS ONE?
DO YOU NOW REVEL IN THE POWER OF YOUR COMBINED STRENGTH?
I LOOK FORWARD TO YOUR ARRIVAL GREATLY, AND THE REJUVENATION IT WILL BRING.
WHEN SHALL IT BE? WHEN SHALL WE THREE MEET AGAIN?
I AM SAD TO REPORT THAT I AM VERY MUCH DIMINISHED IN MY OWN POWERS, AND FIND SUCH THINGS HARDER THAN EVER.
WE LEAVE SOON, THE ARMIES ARE NEARLY READY, THE SUPPLIES ALMOST LOADED.
WE WILL COME WITH ALL HASTE AND JOIN YOU THERE BY THE LAKE, MY SISTER. DO NOT WORRY.

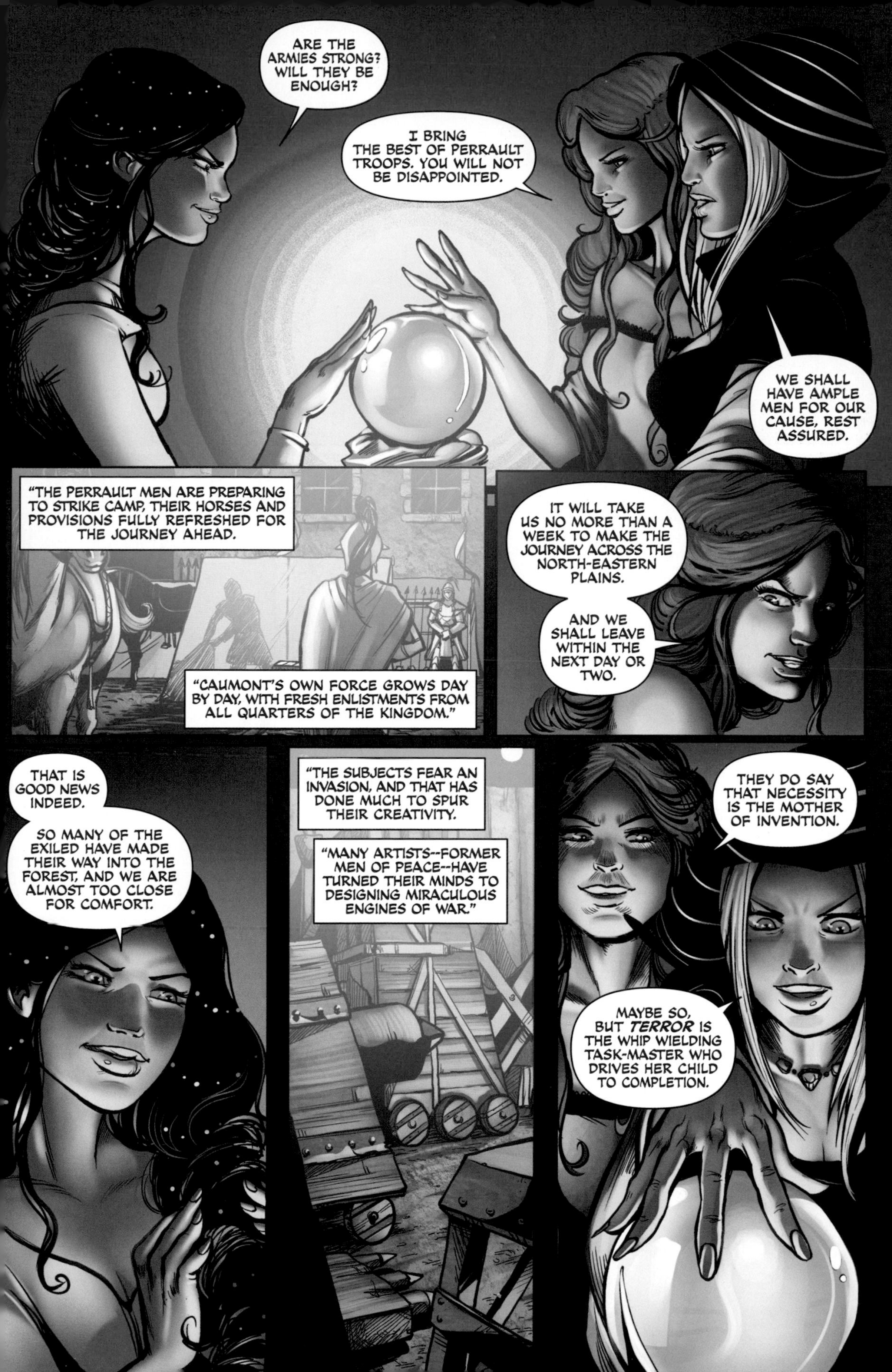
ARE THE ARMIES STRONG? WILL THEY BE ENOUGH?
I BRING THE BEST OF PERRAULT TROOPS. YOU WILL NOT BE DISAPPOINTED.
WE SHALL HAVE AMPLE MEN FOR OUR CAUSE, REST ASSURED.
"THE PERRAULT MEN ARE PREPARING TO STRIKE CAMP, THEIR HORSES AND PROVISIONS FULLY REFRESHED FOR THE JOURNEY AHEAD.
"CAUMONT'S OWN FORCE GROWS DAY BY DAY, WITH FRESH ENLISTMENTS FROM ALL QUARTERS OF THE KINGDOM."
IT WILL TAKE US NO MORE THAN A WEEK TO MAKE THE JOURNEY ACROSS THE NORTH-EASTERN PLAINS.
AND WE SHALL LEAVE WITHIN THE NEXT DAY OR TWO.
THAT IS GOOD NEWS INDEED.
SO MANY OF THE EXILED HAVE MADE THEIR WAY INTO THE FOREST, AND WE ARE ALMOST TOO CLOSE FOR COMFORT.
"THE SUBJECTS FEAR AN INVASION, AND THAT HAS DONE MUCH TO SPUR THEIR CREATIVITY.
"MANY ARTISTS--FORMER MEN OF PEACE--HAVE TURNED THEIR MINDS TO DESIGNING MIRACULOUS ENGINES OF WAR."
THEY DO SAY THAT NECESSITY IS THE MOTHER OF INVENTION.
MAYBE SO, BUT *TERROR* IS THE WHIP WIELDING TASK-MASTER WHO DRIVES HER CHILD TO COMPLETION.

I-I HAVE TO FIND MY FRIEND...
BUT AREN'T WE YOUR FRIENDS NOW, MY LOVELY? ARE WE SUCH TERRIBLE HOSTS AS ALL THAT?
I THINK YOU ARE NOW TRYING TO HURT MY FEELINGS.

AH! THE WINE! EXCELLENT TIMING AS ALWAYS, HEINRICH!

OH!

I'M SO SORRY, MY LADY! I'M SO CLUMSY!
IF YOU HAD DRUNK THE WINE YOU WOULD HAVE BEEN TRAPPED HERE, MY LADY.
YOU CAN TRUST ME. ASK ME TO DANCE.

HEINRICH, YOU STUPID CLUMSY FROG!
YOU DID THIS ON PURPOSE DIDN'T YOU? I KNEW--

THERE'S NO HARM DONE.
I SHOULD LIKE TO DANCE AGAIN, AND TO SHOW THERE'S NO ILL FEELING, I SHOULD LIKE TO DANCE WITH YOU, HEINRICH!
IT WOULD BE AN *HONOUR* MY LADY.

THEY MAKE ME FETCH THE WINE, BECAUSE THAT'S HOW THEY TRAPPED ME HERE.
HAVE YOU HEARD TELL OF THE TWELVE DANCING PRINCESSES? I WAS A SUITOR WHO FOLLOWED THEM.

"I SPAT OUT THE DRUGGED WINE THE PRINCESS OFFERED ME, AND PRETENDED TO BE ASLEEP.
"WHEN THEIR SECRET STAIRWAY WAS REVEALED, I CREPT AFTER THEM.

"FOOLISHLY, I THEN ACCEPTED A DRINK HERE, AT THE DANCE.
"I DID NOT KNOW IT WOULD CURSE ME TO THIS RIDICULOUS FORM, NOR THIS IGNOBLE FATE."

I CAN SHOW YOU HOW TO ESCAPE. BUT YOU MUST MAKE ME A SOLEMN PROMISE.
YOU MUST TAKE ME WITH YOU, AND HAVE ME AS YOUR TRAVELLING COMPANION THEREAFTER.

IF YOU CAN GET US OUT, I SWEAR YOU CAN TRAVEL WITH ME AS LONG AS YOU LIKE.

THEN LET US DANCE THAT WAY, AND BE QUICK BEFORE THEY NOTICE.
WHEN I SAY "RUN" WE GO, AGREED?

"RUN."

DID YOU HEAR THAT? SOUNDED LIKE...

...MARCHING.

THEY'VE SENT IN THE MILITIA! MORE HUMANS TO MAIM. HOW NICE OF THEM!

MY PEOPLE, MY LOYAL CITIZENS OF CAUMONT, IT SADDENS ME TO FIND YOU THUS ENGAGED.

WHEN I SPOKE OF ENEMIES AMONG US, I DID NOT FOR ONE MOMENT MEAN CAUMONT'S DWARVES.

DWARVES *BUILT* THE VERY FOUNDATIONS OF CAUMONT, SHOULDER TO SHOULDER WITH HUMANS, USING DWARVEN TOOLS, AND DWARVEN STONE.

YET, NOW, I FIND DWARVES ***ATTACKING*** HUMANS SAVAGELY. REBELLING FEROCIOUSLY AND WITHOUT CAUSE!

I CANNOT TELL YOU HOW ASHAMED THIS MAKES ME. HOW IT TEARS AT MY HEART TO HEAR OF MEN OF CAUMONT FIGHTING IN THE STREET LIKE DOGS.

I LOVE YOU, AS A FATHER DOES HIS CHILDREN, EVEN WHEN THEY FIGHT, AND STIR UP TROUBLE AMONGST THEMSELVES.

IT IS FOR THIS REASON THAT I SHALL PUT AN *END* TO THIS NOW, AND SHALL TAKE IT NO FURTHER. NO MAN SHALL BE ARRESTED, NOR ANY DWARF.

I DO NOT SEE I HAVE ANY CHOICE BUT TO ASK THE DWARVES OF CAUMONT TO LEAVE, FOR GOOD.

GO BACK TO THE MOUNTAIN VILLAGES OF YOUR ANCESTORS, AND STRIKE THE NAME OF CAUMONT FROM YOUR HEARTS.

IF YOU DO THIS, I GRANT YOU AMNESTY FROM ANY FURTHER REPRISAL OR PROSECUTION.

And so it was, after so many centuries, that the dwarves were banished from Caumont.

WHY IS SO MUCH OF MY TIME SPENT RUNNING THESE DAYS?
NOT JUST RUNNING EITHER, BUT RUNNING *AWAY* FROM THINGS!
THEY'RE RIGHT BEHIND US, BY THE WAY, SO IF YOU HAVE SOMETHING CLEVER IN MIND, I'D SAY LET'S DO IT NOW!

WHUP!
THIS WAY! HURRY!

HOW DID WE GET OUT HERE?
IS THIS ALL UNDERGROUND STILL?
THERE'S NO TIME! PUSH THE BOATS OUT! ALL OF THEM!

HURRY! THEY WILL NOT BE FAR BEHIND US!
DON'T GO IN THE WATER, WHATEVER YOU DO, STAY ON THE SHORE.
WHY? I CAN SWIM OKAY, AND I'M SURE YOU...WELL, I MEAN...

"NO, THERE ARE THINGS IN THERE.
"SLEEPING THINGS THAT DON'T LIKE TO BE WAKED."

HURRY! THEY ARE COMING! I CAN SEE THEM!
COME ON! FOR THE GODS' SAKE! WHAT'S WRONG WITH YOU?

THEY ARE ON US! HURRY!

THAT'S IT! THAT'S IT! NOW *JUMP!* GET IN!

NO! THE FROG AND THE HUMAN!
THEY MUST NOT LEAVE! THEY CANNOT ESCAPE!

STOP! STOP! WE HAVE YOU! WE SHALL KEEP YOU! STOP!

GODS, WHAT ARE THOSE THINGS?
MERMAIDS.
THE LAKE'S FULL OF THEM.

MERMAIDS?

YOUR MAJESTY.

FORGIVE ME, YOUR HIGHNESS. I KNOCKED, BUT YOU WERE SO ABSORBED IN YOUR WORK...
I DID NOT MEAN TO STARTLE YOU.
YOU DID NOT STARTLE ME, COMMANDER SCHWARZ. NOW, WHAT IS IT THAT YOU WANT?

I WISHED TO ASK IF YOU TRULY BELIEVE THAT THIS--THE GREAT WAR TO COME--IS REALLY WHAT HIS HIGHNESS THE KING WOULD WANT.

WHAT DID YOU SAY?

I SAID, ARE YOU SURE THE KING WANTS A WAR?
I MEAN TO SAY, IS HE REALLY SURE OF *ANYTHING* THESE DAYS, YOUR MAJESTY?
HOW *DARE* YOU?

I COULD HAVE YOU *EXECUTED* FOR SUCH TREASON!
YOU DOUBT THE KING? YOU DOUBT *ME?*
YOU THINK I *ENJOY* RULING ALONE WHILE MY HUSBAND IS UNWELL? IS THAT IT?

YOU STILL BELIEVE THAT YOU LOVE HIM, THEN?
WH-WHAT?
WHO ARE YOU?
NO!
TRUE LOVE CURES ALL.
YOUR LOVE IS HIS *CURSE.*
HE WILL NEVER BE FREE.
YOU SHALL *PERISH* ALONE.
YOUR MAJ--
WHAT IN THE NAMES OF THE GODS?
FOREST SPIES!
DID THEY HARM YOU, YOUR HIGHNESS?
YOUR HIGHNESS?

I CAN'T BELIEVE THEY WERE *MERMAIDS!* I'D NO IDEA THEY WERE SO...VICIOUS!
THEY HAVE EATEN THE OTHER LIFE IN THE LAKE, AND ANYTHING WHICH STRAYS TOO CLOSE.
THEY NEST THERE IN THE SHALLOW WATER. HUNDREDS OF THEM.
THE FAIRIES WILL STILL COME AFTER US, WON'T THEY? WHEN THEY GET THEIR BOATS BACK?
THEY CANNOT PASS THE EDGE OF THE LAKE. IT'S PART OF THE ENCHANTMENT.
I WOULD ALSO REMAIN BOUND THERE, HAD YOU NOT RESCUED ME.
I HAVE MADE IT MANY TIMES TO THIS SHORE, YET NEVER WALKED AMONG THESE TREES.
I'D HARDLY CALL IT A *RESCUE* REALLY, I MEAN YOU DID ALL THE--
WHAT'S HAPPENING? WHAT *IS* THIS THING?
MM?
I PICKED IT UP BY THE BOATS. IT JUST LOOKED TOO PRETTY TO LEAVE LYING AROUND.
THIS LAKE IS LINKED TO THE SEA, SO MAYBE IT WAS WASHED IN HERE SOMEHOW.
FLOTSAM AND JETSAM OF ALL KINDS END UP ON THAT SHORE.
US FOR A START.

PAT TAT TAT

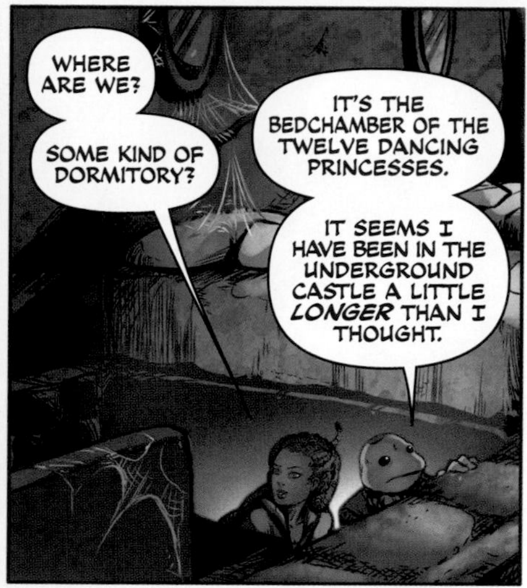
WHERE ARE WE?
SOME KIND OF DORMITORY?
IT'S THE BEDCHAMBER OF THE TWELVE DANCING PRINCESSES.
IT SEEMS I HAVE BEEN IN THE UNDERGROUND CASTLE A LITTLE LONGER THAN I THOUGHT.

THERE THEY ARE, TWELVE OF THE MOST BEAUTIFUL PRINCESSES IN THE WORLD, CAPTURED IN THEIR PRIME.
I BELIEVE IT WAS YOU WHO WAS CAPTURED IN YOUR PRIME, HEINRICH, AND WASN'T IT THEIR FAULT?

IT WAS MY OWN FAULT FOR BELIEVING I COULD JUST STROLL DOWN THERE AND WALK OUT AGAIN.
YEAH, BUT IF THEY HADN'T BEEN SNEAKING OUT TO GO DANCING ALL NIGHT IN THE FIRST PLACE...

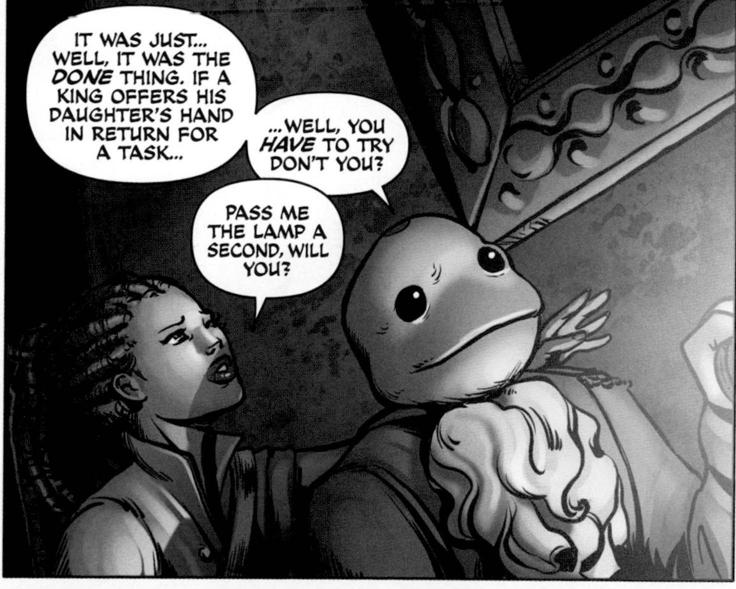
IT WAS JUST... WELL, IT WAS THE DONE THING. IF A KING OFFERS HIS DAUGHTER'S HAND IN RETURN FOR A TASK...
...WELL, YOU HAVE TO TRY DON'T YOU?
PASS ME THE LAMP A SECOND, WILL YOU?

WHO IS THAT?
STOP THAT WOMAN!
BECAUSE YOU'RE THE *REAL* RAPUNZEL.
WHO *IS* THAT?
THAT'S THE QUESTION, ISN'T IT?

Chapter
4

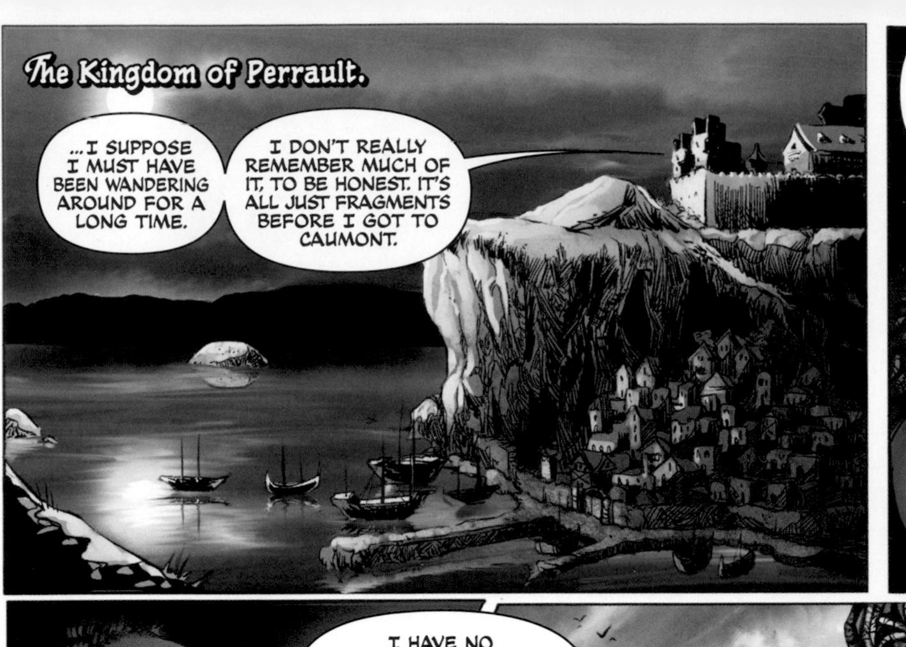
The Kingdom of Perrault.
...I SUPPOSE I MUST HAVE BEEN WANDERING AROUND FOR A LONG TIME.
I DON'T REALLY REMEMBER MUCH OF IT, TO BE HONEST. IT'S ALL JUST FRAGMENTS BEFORE I GOT TO CAUMONT.

I SAW QUEEN TALIA AND KING AURORE ARRIVING THERE. SHE SENT HER GUARDS AFTER ME.
WHICH MEANS SHE RECOGNIZED ME, AND THAT SHE WASN'T HAPPY TO SEE ME.

I HAVE NO MEMORY OF MEETING HER PREVIOUSLY, SO EITHER IT WAS MISTAKEN IDENTITY, OR SHE KNOWS SOMETHING I DON'T.
THEN, IN THE NICK OF THE TIME, I WAS RESCUED BY A STRANGE GIRL.
THE GIRL TURNED OUT TO BE A MERMAID, WHO WAS CONVINCED THAT I'M ACTUALLY QUEEN RAPUNZEL, UNDER A POWERFUL ENCHANTMENT.
SHE INSISTED MY TATTOOS ARE MY WAY OF TRYING TO REMIND MYSELF.

SO, IF SHE'S RIGHT, AND I AM QUEEN RAPUNZEL, THEN WHY WOULD QUEEN TALIA REACT LIKE THAT?
IS SHE AN IMPOSTER? IS THE REAL TALIA OUT THERE SOMEWHERE, LIKE ME?
DOES THAT SOUND MAD?

WHO THIS RAPUNZEL IS, I KNOW NOT.
HOWEVER, IF YOU ARE EXPECTING ME TO DOUBT YOUR STORY ON GROUNDS OF STRANGENESS, YOU ARE PERHAPS OVERLOOKING THE PECULIARITIES OF OUR MEETING...
...AND OUR CURRENT SITUATION.

With the Perrault Royals absent, the girl and the frog spent hours secretly searching the castle's many rooms.
They slept a little when they could, took food from the kitchens.

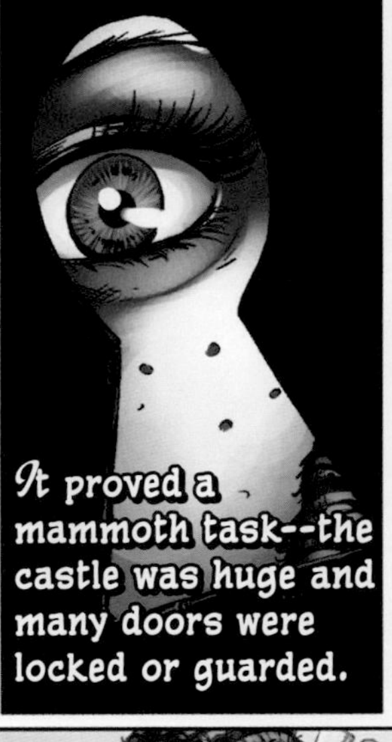
It proved a mammoth task--the castle was huge and many doors were locked or guarded.

If the Queen was an imposter, they could find no proof of it.
For a night and a day they searched, high and low, until they had one narrow escape too many. Neither wished to be caught.

They agreed to leave discretely before daybreak, and seek their answers elswhere.

Perhaps the answer lay in Perrault itself, in the valley below.
As she ran, Rapa felt a sense of purpose for the first time in a long while.

SHE HAS TO BE HERE, HEINRICH. SOMEWHERE DOWN THERE IS THE REAL TALIA, I'M SURE OF IT.
I SHAN'T BE MUCH HELP, I FEAR, LOOKING AS UNUSUAL AS I DO.
She had a goal now, a puzzle to solve, and would not rest until she did so.

WE'LL FIND YOU A CLOAK OF SOME KIND, IT'LL BE FINE.
TO BE HONEST, THE REACTION I GET MOST PLACES, I MAY AS WELL BE A BLOODY FROG.
NO OFFENSE.

"PEOPLE SEEM TO HATE ANYONE *DIFFERENT.*"
WAAAAAH
WAAAAAH
Enchanted Forest.
Daybreak.
WAAAAAH
WAAAAAH
WAAAAAH
WAAAAAH
GOT 'EM! FILTHY BEGGARS!
EEEEEE
THANKS FOR THE HELP, LOVE.
COULDN'T 'AVE DONE IT WITHOUT BAIT.
YOU SHOULD COME TOO, Y'KNOW, IT'S A DANGEROUS PLACE, THIS.

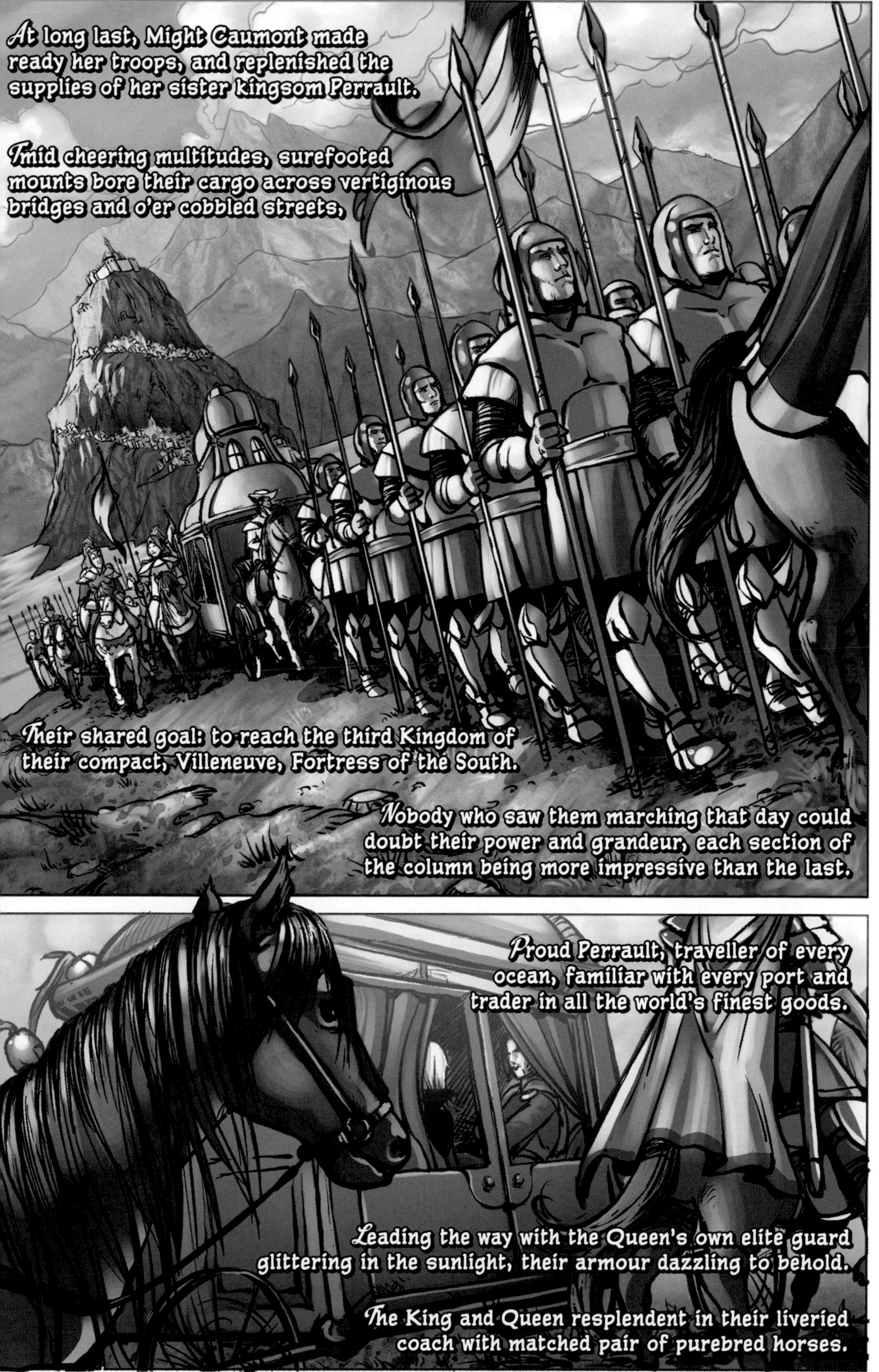
At long last, Might Caumont made ready her troops, and replenished the supplies of her sister kingsom Perrault.
Amid cheering multitudes, surefooted mounts bore their cargo across vertiginous bridges and o'er cobbled streets,
Their shared goal: to reach the third Kingdom of their compact, Villeneuve, Fortress of the South.
Nobody who saw them marching that day could doubt their power and grandeur, each section of the column being more impressive than the last.
Proud Perrault, traveller of every ocean, familiar with every port and trader in all the world's finest goods.
Leading the way with the Queen's own elite guard glittering in the sunlight, their armour dazzling to behold.
The King and Queen resplendent in their liveried coach with matched pair of purebred horses.

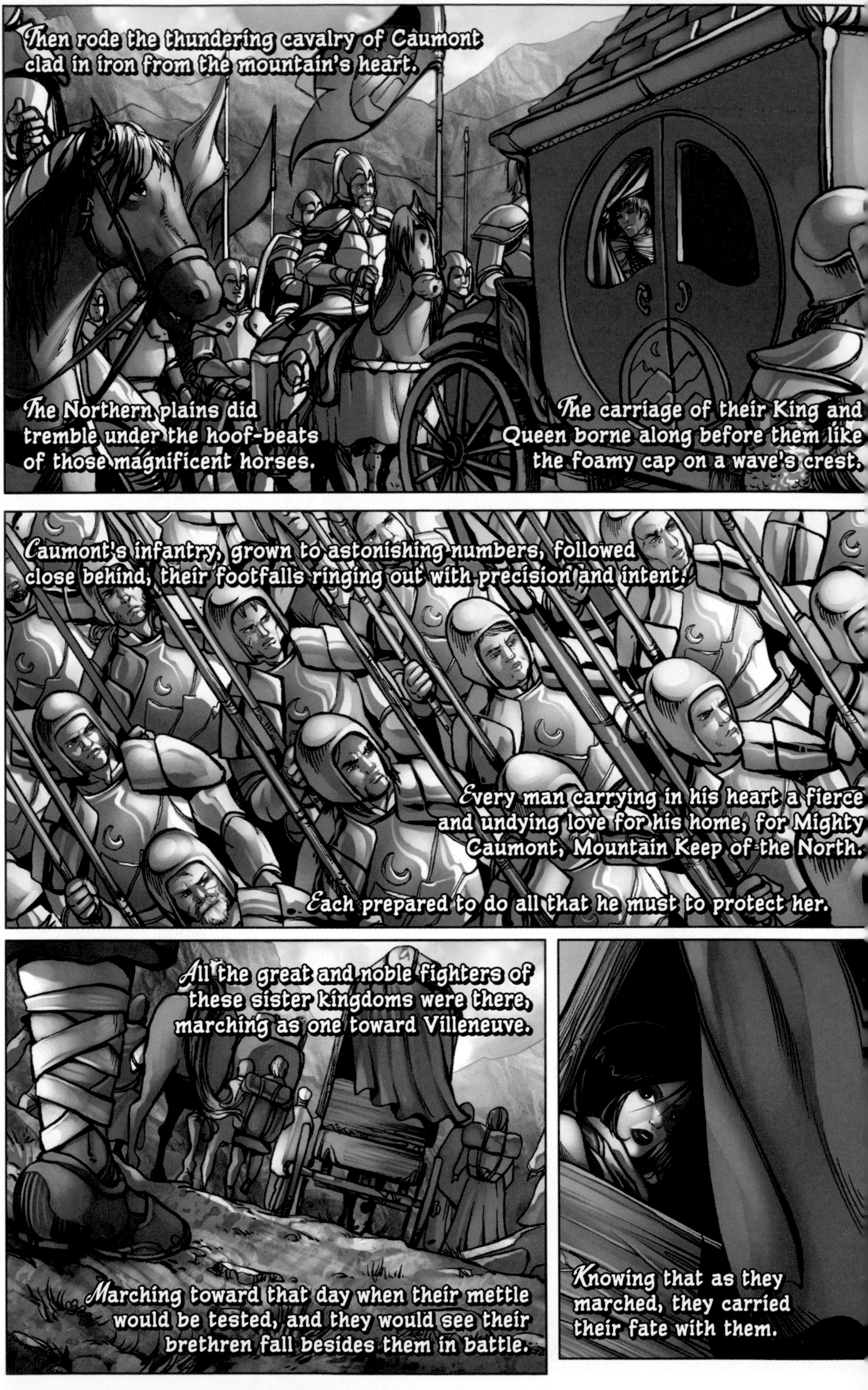

Then rode the thundering cavalry of Caumont clad in iron from the mountain's heart.

The Northern plains did tremble under the hoof-beats of those magnificent horses.

The carriage of their King and Queen borne along before them like the foamy cap on a wave's crest.

Caumont's infantry, grown to astonishing numbers, followed close behind, their footfalls ringing out with precision and intent.

Every man carrying in his heart a fierce and undying love for his home, for Mighty Caumont, Mountain Keep of the North.

Each prepared to do all that he must to protect her.

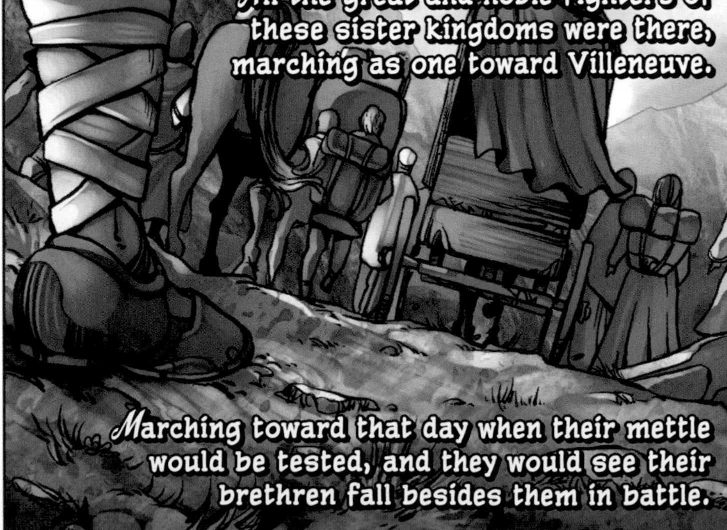

SO, I SUPPOSE THERE'S NOTHING ELSE FOR IT, REALLY. WE'LL JUST HAVE TO TRY TO KEEP AS INCONSPICUOUS AS WE CAN, AND SEARCH THE KINGDOM.
I WISH THERE WAS AN EASIER WAY TO DO ALL THIS. WE DON'T EVEN KNOW IF THE OTHER TALIA'S HERE. OR EVEN IF THERE *IS* ANOTHER TALIA, REALLY...
WELL, WE'VE GOT TO TRY, EH, RAPA?
HA, YES. NOTHING ELSE WE CAN DO, REALLY.
THINK ABOUT IT, *SOMETHING* HAS PROPELLED YOU HERE. SOMETHING WANTS YOU TO FIND THE TRUTH, WANTS YOU TO GO FURTHER.
I BET WHICHEVER WAY WE GO, THAT SOMETHING WILL STEER US RIGHT.
OH, I BET IT WILL! YOU KNOW WHAT THAT *SOMETHING* IS? IT'S A BLOODY *HEX!* I CAN'T GO ANYWHERE WITHOUT SOMETHING AWFUL HAPPENING TO ME.
IT'S LIKE I'M A MAGNET FOR EVERY HUGE, HORRIBLE MONSTER THERE IS! TROLLS, GIANT WORMS, EVIL FAIRIES. YOU NAME IT, IT WANTS TO GET ME.
I'M SURE THAT'S NOT--*UH!*
AAAGH
KRUMMP

NOW, DO YOU SEE WHAT I MEAN?
I-I, *UH,* TAKE YOUR POINT. CERTAINLY.
THE TIMING IS REMARKABLE.
STILL, IT COULD JUST BE SOME KIND OF... COINCIDENCE?
COINCIDENCE...?
"MY GODS, IT'S RIPPING THE CLIFF TO PIECES!"

SIR, I-I THINK YOU SHOULD COME AND SEE THIS, SIR.
I-IT'S SOME OF THE LADS, SIR, THEY'VE GONE A BIT FAR.
FAR? WHAT DO YOU MEAN FAR?
IT'S BETTER IF YOU COME AND SEE, SIR.
GO ON! GIVE IT TO 'EM!
DIRTY LITTLE BEGGARS!
LET ME THROUGH, MAN. GET OUT OF THE WAY.
THEY CAN'T REALLY FEEL NUFFIN', THEY'RE ONLY MADE OF WOOD!
YOU THERE, MAN! WHAT DO THINK YOU'RE DOING? SPEAK!
SIR! COMMANDER SCHWARTZ, SIR!
INFORMATION GATHERING, SIR!
IT'S THE IRON, SIR. THEY HATES THE TOUCH OF IT!

EEEEE
SEE? IT'S NOT EVEN WARM, BUT THEY STILL CRINGE FROM IT!

YOU BARELY NEED TO TOUCH 'EM, SIR, LOOK.

GIVE ME THAT!
WHU?
WHAT SORT OF INFORMATION WERE YOU SUPPOSED TO BE GATHERING?

YOU SPEAK THEIR LANGUAGE, DO YOU?
THESE *THINGS* ARE LITTLE MORE THAN ANIMALS!

YOU'RE TORTURING PATHETIC, HELPLESS CREATURES.

IF YOU WANTED TO GIVE OUR ENEMIES A REASON TO HATE US, YOU'VE DONE A WONDERFUL JOB.
THIS IS NOT A GAME.
CHOKK

CHOKK
THIS IS WAR!

DO YOU UNDERSTAND?
Y-YES, SIR.

GRAAAAK

"I-I MET A MERMAID. SHE DIDN'T HAVE A TAIL. WELL, NOT ON LAND, BUT SHE HAD ONE IN THE WATER.

"MAYBE THAT'S WHAT YOU'RE ALL LIKE...I DON'T REALLY KNOW."

I DON'T KNOW HER NAME, BUT SHE HELPED ME TO ESCAPE QUEEN TALIA'S GUARDS.

SHE SAID WE WERE THE SAME, HER AND I. SAID WE WERE CURSED.

"PLEASE, IF YOU CAN UNDERSTAND ME, PLEASE HELP!"

The Northern Plains.

YOUR MAJESTIES! YOUR MAJESTIES!

WHAT IN ALL THE GODS' NAMES DO *YOU* WANT?
YOUR MAJESTY, A THOUSAND PARDONS FOR DISTURBING YOUR JOURNEY.
I MERELY WONDERED IF THERE WAS ANYTHING I COULD DO FOR YOU. FETCH SOME FOOD, PERHAPS?

YOU IDIOT! YOU SHOULD BE KEEPING OUT OF MY WAY.
YOU ARE LUCKY I HAVE NOT HAD YOU EXECUTED FOR DRAGGING THE KING OFF INTO THE MIDDLE OF A RIOT.

B-BUT YOUR MAJESTY, I--
KING PERSINE IS A SICK MAN. YOUR ACTIONS COULD HAVE *KILLED* HIM!
WHERE WOULD THAT HAVE LEFT ME?
WHERE WOULD IT HAVE LEFT CAUMONT?

GET OUT OF MY SIGHT THIS INSTANT!

THAT *IMBECILE!*
I SHOULD NEVER HAVE ALLOWED YOU TO KEEP AN ADVISOR.

THE BLIND LEADING THE BLIND.
IT MIGHT BE AMUSING IF IT WEREN'T SO TRAGIC.

IT'S MY OWN FAULT, OF COURSE.
I WANTED EVERYTHING TO BE JUST THE WAY IT USED TO BE, BUT THAT JUST IS NOT POSSIBLE. I CAN SEE THAT NOW.

STILL, THERE'S NO HARM DONE.
I JUST NEED TO MAKE SURE THAT I LOOK AFTER YOU PROPERLY FROM NOW ON.

HERE, MY DEAR, IT IS TIME FOR YOUR INFUSION.
OH! THANK YOU, MY LOVE.

GRUHRR

KASPLASH

HELP! PLEASE, HELP US!

GRAAAK

GREEEE
≠COUGH≠ ≠COUGH≠
THEY SAVED US. ≠COUGH≠
THEY LURED IT AWAY.

HEINRICH? IT'S OKAY! WE MADE IT!
CAN YOU HEAR ME? ARE YOU OKAY?

HEINRICH?
YOU'RE A FROG! YOU CAN'T DROWN!

OH GODS, MAYBE IF I...

NO. I'M SORRY. I JUST CAN'T DO IT.
IT'S NOTHING PERSONAL, I JUST UGH I CAN'T!

A-AT LEAST I CAN TRY AND MAKE YOU COMFORTABLE.
KRAK

OH, THE *BOTTLE!*

FIRST I LET YOU DROWN AND THEN I CRACK A BOTTLE OPEN WITH YOUR HEAD!
OH, HEINRICH, PLEASE WAKE UP!
FSSSH

I AM THE JINNI OF THE BOTTLE.
WHOSOEVER RELEASES ME SHALL BE GRANTED WISHES THREE.
TH-THREE WISHES? REALLY?

WELL, I-I WISH HEINRICH WOULD WAKE UP AND BE ALRIGHT.

DONE.
WHAT IS YOUR SECOND WISH?

BLEURGH
HEINRICH! YOU'RE ALIVE!
HEINRICH, THERE'S A JINNI. YOU BROKE THE BOTTLE. WE HAVE THREE WISHES!

TWO WISHES.

OF COURSE. RIGHT.
I WISH YOU WOULD... TAKE US TO WHERE THE REAL TALIA IS!

"DONE."

GOOD MORNING, MY LOVE.
ARE YOU WELL TODAY?
MORNING, IS IT? WHAT DOES IT MATTER TO ME?
LEAVE ME BE, WOMAN.

COME NOW, THAT'S NO GOOD. YOU CAN GET BETTER, MY LOVE, IF YOU REALLY *TRY.*
WON'T YOU TRY? FOR ME, LOVE.
HOW CAN I TRY? HOW CAN I MAKE MYSELF BETTER?

IF YOU SET YOUR MIND TO IT, YOU WON'T FEEL SO BAD...I PROMISE.
THERE'S NOTHING YOU CAN'T DO IF YOU BELIEVE.
I BELIEVE IN YOU.

YOU DO, DO YOU? YOU BELIEVE IN THIS MONSTROUS WRECK?
THEN TRULY YOU ARE AS DOOMED AS I.
THERE IS NO HOPE HERE ANYMORE. NONE AT ALL.

BUT I CAN *GIVE* YOU HOPE, MY LOVE! I CAN GIVE YOU ANYTHING YOU WANT, *EVERYTHING!*
YOU JUST HAVE TO TRUST ME. JUST LOVE ME AND LET ME IN!

SO, IT IS THAT *EASY?* I CAN LOVE YOU AND ALL *THIS,* ALL MY TROUBLES WILL BE *OVER?*
SO, I JUST TURN AND TAKE YOU IN MY ARMS...
MY LOVE, IT IS! IT TRULY IS! IF YOU COULD ONLY KNOW!

MAYBE IT'S TRUE. MAYBE I *CAN* TRUST AGAIN.
MAYBE YOU ARE THE *KEY*, THE LYNCHPIN. IF I CAN TRUST YOU...IF I CAN *LEARN* TO LOVE...
OH, MY LOVE, I WILL TEACH YOU!
THEN WHY DOES MY HEART NOT SWELL AT THOSE WORDS? WHY DOES IT SAY ONLY *"LIAR"*?
WHEN YOU TALK OF *TRUST*...ALL MY BODY, MY BRUTISH FORM SCREAMS OUT *LIAR!*
YOU! WHO HAVE STOLEN LOVE'S FACE? TAKEN IT AS EASILY AS FOR A MASQUERADE BALL...YOU SPEAK OF *TRUST?*
YOU COME TO ME, SMILING THAT SMILE AND TALKING OF LOVE, WHEN YOU KNOW, YOU KNOW ALL THE TIME THAT IT IS *LIES!*
THIS IS ALL SOME MALICIOUS WICKEDNESS DESIGNED TO DRIVE ME MAD!
YOU ARE NOT MY LOVE. YOU ARE NOT SHE, AND SO *I AM IN HELL!*

WHERE ARE WE? WHERE'S TALIA?
IS THIS SOME TRICK?
NO! NO, I PROMISE! IT IS MY CURSE, I CANNOT CONTROL IT.

I AM BOUND TO TAKE YOU AT YOUR EXACT WORD.
YOUR WISH WAS TO BE TAKEN TO THE *PLACE*, NOT THE PERSON.
I KNEW IT! I KNEW THIS WAS TOO GOOD TO BE TRUE!

HANG ON, HANG ON. YOU SAID IT IS YOUR CURSE? WHAT DO YOU MEAN?

I WAS ONCE A MAN--A SIMPLE FISHERMAN--I WAS TRICKED INTO THE BOTTLE CENTURIES AGO BY A WICKED JINNI. DOOMED TO TAKE HIS PLACE.
YOU'RE ENCHANTED. JUST LIKE I WAS.

YOU MUST USE THE THIRD WISH TO FREE HIM.
BUT, HEINRICH, WE'RE--
WE'RE WHERE TALIA IS! WE'LL FIND HER!

SIGH
I WISH YOU WERE FREE OF YOUR CURSE, JINNI.
A THOUSAND THANKS!
I SHALL NEVER FORGET THIS!

WELL DONE. YOU HAVE DONE A WONDERFUL THING!
YEAH, I'LL REMIND YOU OF THAT WHEN YOU'RE REALLY WISHING I'D ASKED FOR WARM CLOTHES AND DINNER.

I SUPPOSE WE SHOULD START LOOKING THEN.
WHERE ARE WE ANYWAY?

THE ENCHANTED FOREST BY THE LOOK OF IT.
HUNDREDS OF MILES OF UNTOUCHED PRIMEVAL WOODLAND.
CAN YOU SEE THAT TOO? IT LOOKS LIKE A LITTLE HOUSE OF SOME KIND.

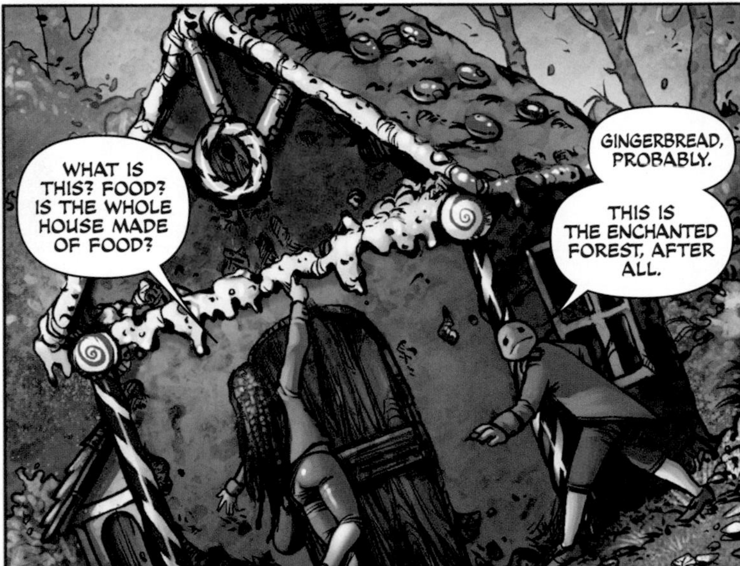
WHAT IS THIS? FOOD? IS THE WHOLE HOUSE MADE OF FOOD?
GINGERBREAD, PROBABLY.
THIS IS THE ENCHANTED FOREST, AFTER ALL.

PTHOOO THIS IS HORRIBLE! IT'S ALL MUSHY!

GAK! I CAN STILL TASTE IT! WHAT KIND OF PERSON HAS A HOUSE MADE OF ROTTEN FOOD?
A WITCH, I'D IMAGINE. WITCHES ARE NOT THE PROBLEM IN HAND, HOWEVER...

...THEY ARE.

"A BABY BEAR...
"...AND A MUMMY BEAR. WHICH ONLY LEAVES..."
...DADDY BEAR!

Chapter 5

Each night, as darkness descends upon the Earth, its sons and daughters prepare to depart their world.
Heads begin to nod, eyelids grow too heavy to raise, familiar sounds echo then tail away.
Sleep comes to the children of Earth.
And in slumber come dreams.
GRIMMS FAIRY T
Dreams of far off lands, uncharted, yet instinctively known.
Of adventures never before undertaken, whose outcome is nevertheless inevitable.
BATTLE FOR
Dreams dreamt for generations, for centuries for aeons.
THE COMPLETE ALICE
Everlasting, ever-changing, every night, for evermore.

One by one, the children awake into an old, old place within the dream.

Instantly at ease within the confines of the warm, sweet-scented Sanctum Somnium, their dream-selves yawn and stretch.

In this Chamber of Dreams, familiar tales are retold night after night.

Story-seeds are planted in the dreamers' imaginations.

And new, though recognizable narratives blossom forth.

The stories grow, they adapt, they live.

Each night a whole world is dreamed into existence.

A world where gryphons guard treasures buried in labryinths of stone beneath shifting desert sands.

Where millennia-old tatsu glide through the air amongst mist-gray mountains, before diving serpents-like into the foam-crested azure ocean.

And where faeries and other-folk dwell in a vast, lush Enchanted Forest.

In the middle of that forest grows a mighty oak more ancient than any other.

Oberon, King of the fa[illegible]ies, lives within its trunk and his fae subjects guard it wel

The dense thickets of the Enchanted Forest are home to a magical multitude inhabiting every nook and cranny.

It's an old story of a dark forest.
Of a pack of hungry wolves on the hunt.
Of a lone figure in a scarlet hooded cloak.
"Where are you going to, Little Red Hood?" say the wolves.
"On your way to Grandma's house perhaps?"
But little Red Hood has heard this story before.
MY, WHAT SMALL BRAINS YOU HAVE!
SWSH SWSH SWSH

AAAGH!
AAUGH! HELP!
GODS DAMN THAT JINNI!
IF TALIA EVER *WAS* HERE, SHE'LL HAVE BEEN EATEN ALIVE BY WILD BEASTS!

AAUGH! HELP!
AAAGH!

GRAAAA
I HOPE YOU CHOKE ON MY HAIR, YOU FURRY SON OF A WITCH!
♫
I SEE IT BUT I DON'T BELIEVE IT. BEARS HUNTING HUMANS...
WHAT HAPPENED? RUN OUT OF PORRIDGE?
OR DID YOU FORGET WHAT I *DO* TO BEASTS THAT EAT *PEOPLE?*
YOU HAVE A CHOICE, BEARS. LEAVE NOW, OR *DIE.*

The Myvathen Mire.
KNOCK
KNOCK
KNOCK
WHO DARES TO...?
OH, IT'S YOU, RAPUNZEL. WHAT IS IT?
WE HAVE COME TO A STOP.
ALTHOUGH, I SEE THAT YOU HAD NOT NOTICED.
WHAT'S THE DELAY?
OUR PASSAGE ACROSS THE MYVATHEN BRIDGE IS BLOCKED.
AN AUDIENCE HAS BEEN REQUESTED.

"GINNY GREENTEETH--THE WITCH OF THE MIRE--DEMANDS TO SPEAK WITH US BEFORE SHE WILL ALLOW ANY TO PASS.
"JUST US, TALIA. NOT THE KINGS.
"SHE WAS QUITE SPECIFIC ABOUT THAT."
VERY WELL, RAPUNZEL. LET US SEE WHAT THE SWAMP HAG HAS TO SAY.
CAREFUL, COUSIN. DO NOT TREAT THIS LIGHTLY.
"IT SEEMS SOME HAVE A GREATER KNOWLEDGE OF OUR AFFAIRS THAN WE HAD ANTICIPATED."

The Enchanted Forest.
Deep within the Great Oak.
YOU'RE NEXT, BROTHERS.
KING OBERON WILL SEE YOU NOW.
YOUR MAJESTY, IT IS A PLEASURE TO MEET YOU.
WE HAVE JOURNEYED FAR, YOUR HIGHNESS, FORCED FROM OUR OWN PLACE, BY THE HATRED OF THE HUMANS.
THE DETESTATION OF OTHER-FOLK SPREADS LIKE A DISEASE THROUGH MANKIND, SIRE. WE COULD BEAR IT NO LONGER.
WE HAVE COME TO OFFER OUR HELP.

I ASK YOU TO RECONSIDER. RETURN TO YOUR HOMELAND, TO YOUR FAMILIES, AND REMAIN HIDDEN.
REMAIN SAFE.
WE WILL NOT. WE KNOW WHAT WE RISK, BUT THE ALTERNATIVE IS FAR WORSE.
WE HAVE COME TO FIGHT, YOUR MAJESTY.
YOU ARE BRAVE INDEED, GOOD GNOMES.
I THANK YOU, AND WELCOME YOU TO OUR RANKS.
I, YOUR KING, AM PROUD OF YOU. OF *ALL* OF YOU!
OUR ENEMIES SEEK TO DRIVE US OUT, BUT INSTEAD THEY BRING US CLOSER TOGETHER. THEY MAKE US STRONGER.
BY THE GODS OF THE GLADE, OF THE FOREST, OF THE DALE, I, OBERON, SWEAR THEY SHALL REGRET DOING SO!

I BEG OF YOU LADIES, LEAVE ME BEHIND. I AM ONLY A HINDRANCE TO YOUR PROGRESS.

HEINRICH, IF YOU CALL US "LADIES" ONE MORE TIME...
DO YOU SEE US SIPPING TEA, OR DOING NEEDLEPOINT?

I DID NOT WISH TO OFFEND, RATHER JUST TO--OUCH! OH DEAR...
SAVE YOUR STRENGTH, FROG. THERE'LL BE TIME TO TALK LATER.

WE'RE HOME.
OH!
NICE PLACE...

THERE, SIT THE FROG ON THE BENCH AND I'LL MAKE A POULTICE.
MADAM, MY NAME IS HEINRICH, AND I DON'T-- *OUCH!* OH DEAR...
COLLECTING STRAYS AGAIN, RED?
I AM TALIA, AND YOU ARE VERY WELCOME TO RODENDORF. WHAT'S LEFT OF IT, ANYWAY.
T-TALIA? YOU'RE TALIA? AS IN *QUEEN TALIA?*
I USED TO BE. A LONG TIME...
MY GODS. *RAPUNZEL?*

MY DARLING QUEEN, IS EVERYTHING ALRIGHT?
WHA? YOU'RE NOT TALIA!
YOU'RE DAMN RIGHT I'M NOT.
PLEASE, DON'T SCREAM. I DON'T WANT TO HURT YOU. WHAT'S THE MATTER? DON'T YOU RECOGNIZE ME?
WHOEVER YOU ARE, I'LL GIVE YOU ANYTHING!
ANYTHING I WANT? YOU REALLY DON'T RECOGNIZE ME, DO YOU?
"I RECOGNIZED YOU, THE VERY FIRST TIME I SAW YOU.
"I KNEW YOU WERE THE ONE. THE ONLY ONE I COULD EVER LOVE.
"YOU WERE SO BEAUTIFUL, LEANING THERE IN THE SUN.
"YOUR FRIEND WAS LAUGHING AT YOU--HOW COULD YOU HOPE TO FIND LOVE WHEN YOU WERE SO PICKY?
"YOU SAID YOU'D FIND HER AT YOUR BIRTHDAY BALL.

"THAT NIGHT, A GREAT STORM BLEW UP, YOUR SHIP WAS THROWN ABOUT LIKE A TOY.
"I SAW YOU ON DECK, DROPPING SAIL. AND I SAW YOU FALL IN.
"THERE YOU WERE, FLOATING WITH YOUR ARMS OUTSTRETCHED. AS IF YOU KNEW I WOULD COME FOR YOU.
"AS IF YOU WANTED *ME* TO SAVE YOU, AND NO-ONE ELSE.
"I WAITED THERE UNTIL THEY FOUND YOU. I WATCHED AS THEY CARRIED YOU AWAY.
"I KNEW I HAD TO GET TO THAT BALL, NO MATTER WHAT THE COST.
"I WENT TO THE SEA WITCH.
"TO WIN YOUR HEART AT THE BALL--TO DANCE--I NEEDED *LEGS.*
"I BEGGED, I PLEADED, UNTIL SHE SAID THERE *WAS* A WAY.
"A POTION WOULD GIVE ME LEGS. WALKING WOULD BE...*UNCOMFORTABLE* ...BUT I'D HAVE LEGS!
"A POTION AND A DAGGER... *THIS* DAGGER I HAVE HERE...
"I DIDN'T HESITATE. I KNEW IT WAS MEANT TO BE.
"YOU WOULD LOVE ME, AND I WOULD BECOME A REAL GIRL, WE'D BE WED, AND I'D BE A *PRINCESS!*
"YOU LOOKED ME UP AND DOWN, ASKED ME TO DANCE RIGHT AWAY.
"DANCING, YOU HELD ME SO CLOSELY. I KNEW YOU LOVED ME TOO.

"YOU DIDN'T PROPOSE THAT NIGHT, BUT INVITED ME TO THE *NEXT* BALL, ONE MONTH HENCE.
"SO I WAITED, FOR THAT WHOLE MONTH, JUST THINKING OF YOU.
"IMAGINING OUR LIFE *TOGETHER*.
"EVENTUALLY, THE TIME PASSED, AND AGAIN I CAME TO THE CASTLE.
"THE WALKING HURT, BUT I THOUGHT ONLY OF YOU.
"WHEN I ARRIVED... I-I THOUGHT THERE WAS SOME MISTAKE.
"THERE WAS NO BALL, IT WAS A *WEDDING! YOUR* WEDDING...TO ANOTHER GIRL!
"I SAW YOU THERE COOING OVER EACH OTHER LIKE TURTLE DOVES, AND COULD ONLY THINK IT WAS A DREAM.
"A STRANGE... *HORRIBLE* DREAM."
THAT WAS IT FOR YOU, WASN'T IT? *"HAPPILY EVER AFTER"*? IS THAT WHAT YOU THINK?
PLEASE, I-I DON'T KNOW WHAT YOU MEAN...
"YOUR *PRECIOUS*, BELOVED WIFE.
"YOU FOOL. SHE'S NOT WHO YOU THINK SHE IS.
"NOT AT ALL."

IT WAS SO LONG AGO, I DIDN'T HAVE A NAME YET.
ON MY NAMING DAY, A WOMAN I DIDN'T EVEN KNOW GAVE ME A DEATH SENTENCE.

MY FATHER INVITED THE WHOLE FOREST--HUMAN AND FAE--EXCEPT FOR ONE OLD CRONE.
SHE ARRIVED ANYWAY, FURIOUS WITH US ALL, AND BESTOWED HER LITTLE "GIFT." SHE PROMISED ME DEATH BY SPINDLE WHEN I TURNED FIFTEEN.

SOME FAIRY TRIED TO HELP, AND MANAGED TO MAKE IT *SLEEP* INSTEAD OF DEATH...
MY FIFTEENTH BIRTHDAY, I FIND MYSELF IN A CASTLE TOWER WITH AN OLD WOMAN SAT SPINNING. IT SOUNDS RIDICULOUS, I KNOW.

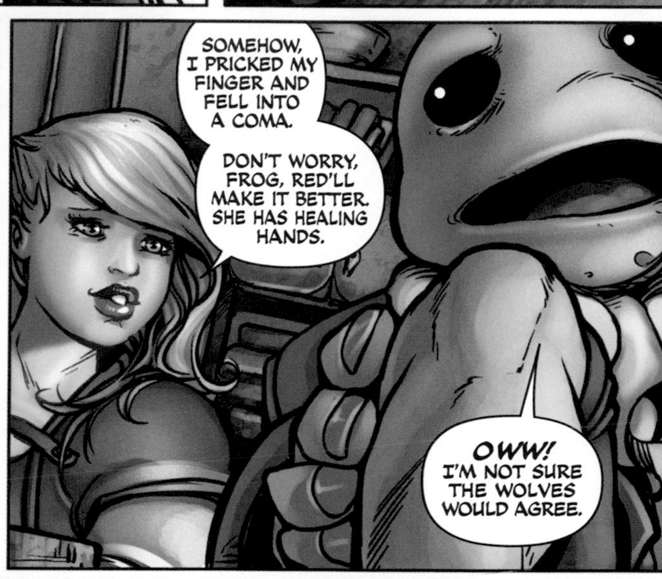
SOMEHOW, I PRICKED MY FINGER AND FELL INTO A COMA.
DON'T WORRY, FROG, RED'LL MAKE IT BETTER. SHE HAS HEALING HANDS.
OWW! I'M NOT SURE THE WOLVES WOULD AGREE.

SO, I FELL ASLEEP, BUT SO DID EVERYONE ELSE.
I STAYED YOUNG, PROTECTED BY THE ENCHANTMENT. BUT EVERYONE ELSE AGED NORMALLY. THEY DIE. THEY *ROT.*

"ONE HUNDRED YEARS LATER, A KISS AWOKE ME, AND I MARRIED PRINCE AURORE OF PERRAULT.
"WHY? MY HOME WAS IN RUINS. MY FAMILY AND FRIENDS ALL DEAD. I WAS *STILL* FIFTEEN.
"WHAT CHOICE DID I HAVE?

"AURORE BECAME KING, MAKING ME THE MOST SCRUTINIZED GIRL IN PERRAULT.
"CRITICISM ON MY WEIGHT, MY LOOKS, MY CLOTHES...AND OF COURSE, WHERE WAS THE HEIR?
"I WAS DAYDREAMING ONE DAY, STARING AT MY OWN REFLECTION, WHEN SUDDENLY THE FACE BEFORE ME WASN'T MY OWN.
"I THOUGHT BOREDOM HAD DRIVEN ME MAD...
"...UNTIL SHE SPOKE."
DON'T WORRY, TALIA, MY DEAR, THIS WON'T HURT A BIT, AND YOU'LL REMEMBER NOTHING.
ALL THAT WAS YOURS IS MINE, AND MINE IT WILL REMAIN.
NO FRIEND SHALL KNOW YOU, BY SIGHT, NOR VOICE.
YOU WILL WANDER THE LAND TO THE END OF YOUR DAYS.
NONE SHALL WELCOME YOU; NONE SHALL BE YOUR FRIEND.
YOU SHALL LIVE ON, AN EMPTY VESSEL, AND REMEMBER NOTHING.
NOT OF YOUR FORMER LIFE, NOR YOUR FORMER SELF.
SPLUTCH
"I DIDN'T KNOW WHO I WAS. OR WHERE.
"OR ANYTHING.

"I WAS DESPERATE, I HAD ONLY THE CLOTHES I STOOD UP IN, AND YET NO-ONE WOULD HELP ME.
"SOMEONE SAID I WAS A THIEF, THEN ANOTHER SAID I'D PUT A HEX ON THEIR CHILDREN.
"IT WAS THE SAME WHEREVER I WENT, PEOPLE TURNED AGAINST ME.
"ALWAYS, THE OUTLANDER COME TO STEAL OR DEFRAUD THEM.
"EVENTUALLY I GAVE UP. I LAY DOWN, AND WAITED FOR DEATH'S COLD CLUTCHES.
"INSTEAD, I FOUND A WARMER EMBRACE.
"STRONG ARMS LIFTED ME FROM MY DEGRADATION.
"HEALING HANDS BATHED MY WOUNDS, AND GAVE ME FOOD."
TRUE LOVE.
ALL ENCHANTMENTS CAN BE BROKEN BY TRUE LOVE.
THE WITCH HAD EITHER FORGOTTEN, OR DIDN'T THINK I'D A HOPE OF FINDING IT.
TRUE LOVE.
TRUE LOVE? I-I DON'T UNDERSTAND. I... I MEAN I JUST ASSUMED...

SLEEPING BEAUTY IS DEAD! THE WITCH CARABOSSE TOOK HER PLACE!
SHE AND HER COVEN HAVE ENCHANTED YOU AND EVERYONE AROUND YOU!
ALL THIS-- THE COMPACT, THE ARMIES, THE WAR--IT'S ALL THEIR PLAN!

BUT I'M HERE TO BREAK THE SPELL, TO MAKE YOU SEE THE TRUTH.
BECAUSE I LOVE YOU! AND I KNOW THAT YOU LOVE ME TOO!

YES...YES, I-I SEE IT NOW...
OF COURSE, YOU'RE RIGHT...MY... MY LOVE.

OH, MY DARLING, I KNOW YOU MUST BE CONFUSED, BUT THAT WILL FADE, I PROMISE.
I'LL TAKE CARE OF YOU, MY LOVE.

WE CAN JUST SLIP AWAY IN THE NIGHT TOGETHER.
ALL WE NEED IS EACH OTHER!

THUNG
GAH! YOU VILE, UGLY THING!

I GAVE UP *EVERYTHING* FOR YOU.
EVERY STEP LIKE WALKING ON BROKEN *GLASS.*
BANISHED FROM THE UNDERSEA KINGDOM *FOREVER!*

BUT, THE SEA WITCH GAVE ME THIS DAGGER. IF I COULDN'T *WIN* YOUR HEART, I SHOULD *TAKE* IT.
FOR *HER!*

AARRRRRGH!

MY GODS! YOUR MAJESTY, WHAT HAS HAPPENED?
...STOP... IT...

...STOP... THAT... *THING*...
QUICKLY! FETCH THE HEALER, HE'S BLEEDING BADLY!
WHAT WAS IT? A *BEAST* PERHAPS?
ONE THING'S CERTAIN; NOTHING *HUMAN* COULD SURVIVE OUT THERE!

WAIT, SO I'M SUPPOSED TO FALL IN LOVE?
JUST FIND A MAN, OR A WOMAN, OR SOMEONE... THAT'S WHAT YOU'RE TELLING ME?

YOUR STORY... I COULD HAVE TOLD IT MYSELF.
YET, MY TATTOOS WERE DONE OVER AND OVER AGAIN!
I FORGET! I ALWAYS FORGET! I WORK IT OUT, I PIECE IT TOGETHER...

I CAN END IT FOR YOU. I THINK I CAN BREAK THE ENCHANTMENT.

YOU ARE RAPUNZEL, THE GIRL IN THE TOWER WITH THE BEAUTIFUL HAIR...
...AND YOU STILL LOVE KING PERSINE.

MY GODS!
PERSINE...

"I LOVE HIM.
"AND THAT... THAT WITCH HAS HIM PRISONER!

"I HAVE TO SAVE HIM!"

Chapter 6

RAPUNZEL! RAPUNZEL!

LET DOWN YOUR HAIR!
IT'S ME, PRINCE PERSINE!

OH, MY LOVE, AT LAST THE EVENING IS HERE.
EACH DAY WITHOUT YOU IS AN ETERNITY.
PERSINE, MY DARLING, HOW IS IT THAT YOU WEIGH SO MUCH LESS THAN MOTHER GOTHEL?
IT TAKES ALL MY STRENGTH TO PULL HER UP EVERY MORNING!
IS THAT SO, MY DEAR? IS THAT SO?
WELL, ISN'T THAT INTERESTING...
LYING, UNGRATEFUL CHILD! SO, THIS IS WHAT YOU DO WHEN MY BACK IS TURNED.
LET DOWN YOUR HAIR, *RAPUNZEL!*

RAPA? RAPA, ARE YOU OKAY?

WE WERE TRYING TO LET YOU SLEEP, BUT THEN, WELL...YOU DIDN'T SEEM VERY *HAPPY.*
HEINRICH IS BEING POLITE, RAPA. YOU WERE SCREAMING BLUE MURDER.

I WAS DREAMING ABOUT RAPUN--ABOUT THE PAST, I SUPPOSE. GODS, BUT IT'S CONFUSING.
IT HAS BEEN BUT A WEEK. GIVE IT TIME, MY LADY.

I REMEMBER VERY LITTLE OF MY OWN FORMER LIFE, MERELY THE EVENTS WHICH LED TO MY BEING CURSED...
WOULD MEMORIES CHANGE ME? OR ARE WE SIMPLY THE PERSON WE ARE NOW, IN THIS MOMENT?

I DIDN'T FEEL LIKE *ME* FOR A LONG TIME. I HAD NO IDEA WHAT WAS. A QUEEN? A WIFE?
I'D NEVER BEEN *ALLOWED* TO FIND OUT WHO I WAS. TAKE YOUR TIME, RAPA.
LET'S EAT. WE HAVE TO LEAVE SOON.

I PROBABLY SHOULD HAVE SAID THIS ALREADY, BUT I OWE YOU ALL, FOR COMING WITH ME LIKE THIS.
THANK YOU.
I HAD BEEN IN THAT GODFORSAKEN PLACE FOR HUNDREDS OF YEARS.
I WOULD HAVE BEEN THERE HUNDREDS MORE.
I OWE YOU MY LIFE. I'LL NOT REST UNTIL I'VE REPAID THAT DEBT.
YOU DON'T OWE *ME* ANYTHING.
I JUST WISH I'D REALIZED SOONER THAT I WASN'T THE ONLY ONE SUFFERING.
I WAS JUST SO HAPPY TO HAVE THAT CURSE BROKEN. TO FINALLY REST, AND NOT BE PERSECUTED.
IT NEVER OCCURRED TO ME THERE MIGHT BE... ***MORE.***
WHICH IS WHY WE NEED TO LEAVE. VILLENEUVE IS TWO DAYS TREK.
TWO DAYS UNTIL THE FINAL PIECE IN THE PUZZLE.
UNTIL WE FIND OUT WHETHER BELLE WAS REPLACED, TOO.

Villeneuve.
GET OUT! GET OUT, I TELL YOU!

TRRRAITOR! WRETCHED TRAITOR! DON'T COME TO ME WITH YOURRR LIES!
GET AAAOOOUT!

RAAAGH
≈SOB≈

BY HEKATE, WHY? WHY?
WHY CAN'T HE JUST LOVE ME?
TRUE LOVE WOULD FIX IT!

IF HE ONLY BELIEVED, HE DOESN'T NEED TO BE A BEAST ANYMORE.
I LOVE HIM, AND I'M HER NOW...I MEAN, I LOOK THE SAME AS...

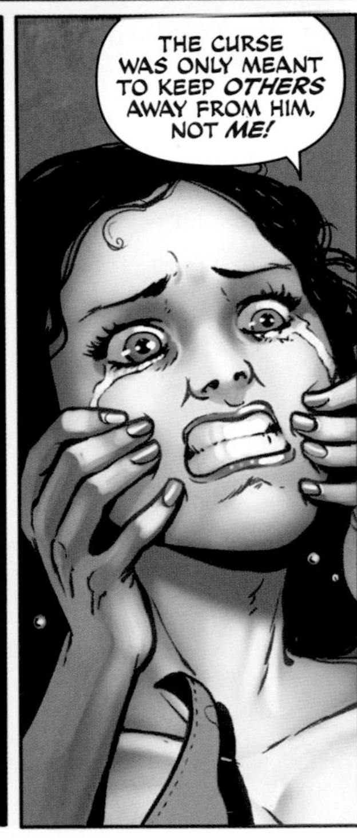
THE CURSE WAS ONLY MEANT TO KEEP OTHERS AWAY FROM HIM, NOT ME!

GOTHEL AND CARABOSSE TOLD ME IT WOULD WORK, THAT I WOULD HAVE HIM, AND I *BELIEVED* THEM.
ALL THEY WANT IS *POWER,* BUT I-I DID IT FOR...OH, IF ONLY HE COULD SEE I DID IT ALL FOR *LOVE!*

AAAH!

EVERYWHERE! THEY'RE *EVERYWHERE!*

LITTLE FLAPPING *CREATURES!* LITTLE SHARP TEETH!
EVERY CORNER, THERE THEY ARE... *WATCHING!*
IS THERE NOWHERE SAFE? NOWHERE I CAN HIDE FROM THEM?
IS THERE NOWHERE WE COULD GO...JUST ME AND *HIM?* TOGETHER?

HANDS REACH OUT ACROSS TIME AND SPACE. HEAR MY CALL!
ANSWER ME! WE NEED YOU!

BELLADONNA, WE ARE UNDER ATTACK!
HEAR MY CALL!

The Eastern edge of the Enchanted Forest, ten leagues North-West of Villeneuve.

BAH! FOOLISH OLD ENCHANTRESS!

WHERE IS SHE? OFF FUSSING OVER THAT *THING* SHE CALLS A HUSBAND?

MEDDLING DRYADS!

THEY ARE MERE WOOD!

AXES! FETCH AXES!

FELL THEM ALL!

BUILD A BONFIRE!

"DID THE WITCH EVER WHISPER TO YOU?
"TELL YOU...STORIES?"
THE WITCH CARABOSSE THOUGHT I WAS DEAD. SHE DIDN'T KNOW HER CURSE HAD FAILED UNTIL I AWOKE.
W-WHY WOULD SHE TELL ME *STORIES?*
"I... I THINK I CAN REMEMBER MOTHER GOTHEL TELLING ME STORIES. IN THE TOWER.
"ABOUT HERSELF, HOW POWERFUL SHE WAS...AND ALL THE EVIL THINGS SHE DID OUT THERE IN THE BLACK OF NIGHT."
AND THEN I'D DREAM, AND THE NEXT DAY SHE'D *KNOW,* AND WOULD SAY SHE'D *DONE* THE THINGS I DREAMED.
...SOARED ON BATWINGS, CLAWED OPEN COFFINS TO STEAL MAGICAL AMULETS...
PERHAPS YOUR DREAMS, YOUR BELIEF, YOUR FEAR...PERHAPS SHE NEEDED THAT?

Villeneuve.
"THERE! I SEE THEM. THEY MUST BE A DAY NOR-WEST OF HERE. WHERE THE TRACK SKIRTS THE FOREST.
"I CAN'T MAKE OUT WHAT IS HAPPENING, BUT THERE'S FIRE AND A GOOD DEAL OF SMOKE."
THERE! I SEE ARMOUR SHINING. IT'S THEM!
QUICK, LAD! TELL SCHWARTZ! RUN!
YOUR MAJESTY! THE CARAVAN IS UNDER ATTACK!
BUT HOW...?
W-WHATEVER DO YOU MEAN?
THEY'VE BEEN AMBUSHED ON THE EDGE OF THE ENCHANTED FOREST.
IT'S A DAY'S RIDE, BUT IF WE USE THE ENGINES OF WAR *HERE*--
NO.
BUT, YOUR MAJESTY...
WE WILL LAUNCH NO ATTACK. I HAVE CHANGED MY MIND.
YOUR... YOUR MAJESTY PLEASE, THINK WHAT THE KING WOULD WANT YOU TO DO...
NO! AWAY FROM ME! OUT!
OUT!

COMMANDER SCHWARTZ, SIR.
WHAT DID THE QUEEN SAY, SIR?
WHAT DO YOU *THINK* SHE SAID, SOLDIER?
"THE ENEMY HAS STRUCK THE FIRST BLOW.
"OUR ALLIES ARE UNDER ATTACK.
"SOUND THE CALL.
"WE GO TO WAR!"

WE SHOULD BE BACK *THERE.* WE SHOULD BE CLAWING AND PECKING THOSE HUMAN--
THE DRYADS SHOULD NOT HAVE ATTACKED.
NEVERTHELESS, THE WAR IS BEGUN.
AND *ENDED,* IF THE TREE-FOLK WIN!
EVEN WITH THE ELEMENT OF SURPRISE THEY ARE HOPELESSLY OUTNUMBERED.
FIRE AND IRON WILL DO FOR THEM SOON ENOUGH, I'M AFRAID.
WE MUST GET WORD TO KING OBERON. HE MUST KNOW WHAT HAS HAPPENED.
FMP
BALLS!

Eastern outskirts of the Enchanted Forest, near Villeneuve.
WHUD
RUMMBLE
WHRRR
RRRUMMMBLE

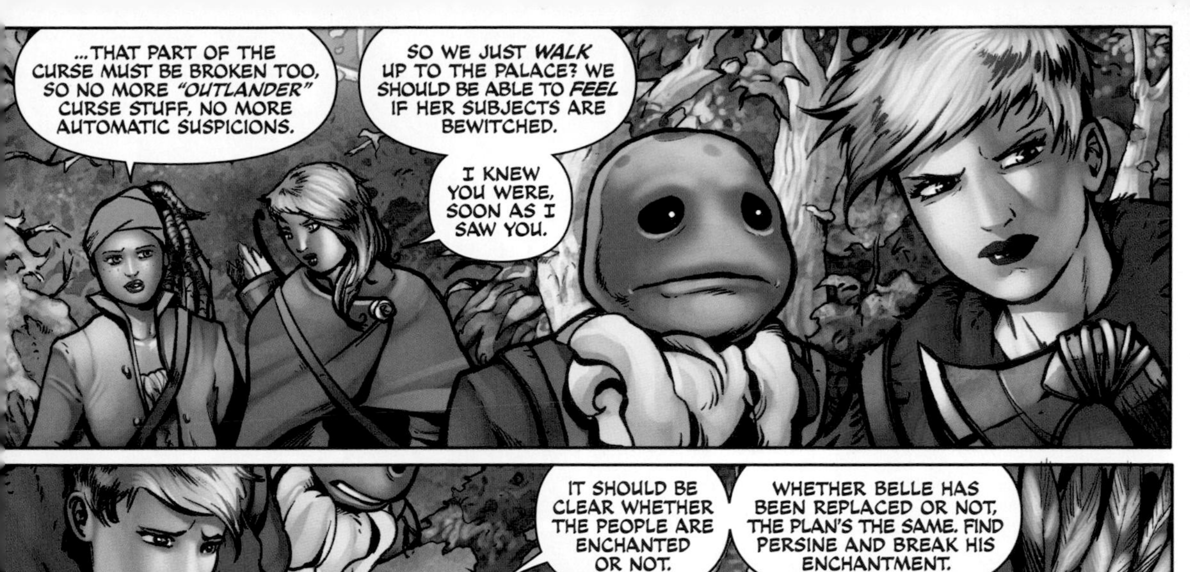
...THAT PART OF THE CURSE MUST BE BROKEN TOO, SO NO MORE "OUTLANDER" CURSE STUFF, NO MORE AUTOMATIC SUSPICIONS.
SO WE JUST WALK UP TO THE PALACE? WE SHOULD BE ABLE TO FEEL IF HER SUBJECTS ARE BEWITCHED.
I KNEW YOU WERE, SOON AS I SAW YOU.

IT SHOULD BE CLEAR WHETHER THE PEOPLE ARE ENCHANTED OR NOT.
WHETHER BELLE HAS BEEN REPLACED OR NOT, THE PLAN'S THE SAME. FIND PERSINE AND BREAK HIS ENCHANTMENT.

HEINRICH, LOOK AT THIS: IT'S IRON.

SOMETHING'S WRONG HERE.

KANNG

FRIEND OR...UH, FOE?
I COULD ASK YOU THE SAME.
BUT FRIENDS I HAVE ALREADY.
PEOPLE SNEAKING UP ON US? USUALLY FOES.
HOLD!
LOWER YOUR BLADE, MASTER THISTLEDOWN.
PLEASE, GOOD PEOPLE, WE MEAN YOU NO HARM.
YOU AND YOUR COMPANIONS HAVE JOURNEYED FAR FROM THE RIVER LANDS, BROTHER FROG.
NAPAIOS, LOOK! IT-IT'S RUNCIBLE! HE'S...
THAT WASN'T US!
THAT BALL THING WAS ALREADY HERE!
HOW WILL WE TELL MADAME PUSSYCAT?
I HAVE HEARD TALK OF IRON MISSILES FROM THE FAIRIES. THIS HAS COME FROM VILLENEUVE.
IT IS BEGUN THEN.
COME, FRIENDS, THERE IS NO TIME TO LOSE.
WE MUST WARN KING OBERON.
WAIT, DID YOU SAY VILLENEUVE?

PLEASE NOOOOO!
HA-HA-HAAA!
READY...
FIRE!
GAH! PIXIE-SHOT!

⫶UNGH⫶
ENOUGH! YOUR TRICKS DON'T WORK ON ME, YOU MAGIC SCUM!
KFFFT
WHA?
⫶CHOKE⫶
NO HARM CAN COME TO YOU NOW.
YOU ARE AS ONE WITH THE ENCHANTED FOREST.
"...STARTED THE WAR...
"...KNOCKED RUNCIBLE OUT OF THE AIR...
"...GOT TO TELL KING OBERON..."

The Great Oak.
...GOT TO TELL THE KING...
...DRYADS ATTACKED THE HUMANS...
...STARTED THE WAR...
I'VE GOT TO SEE KING OBERON!
NOHOW!
CONTRARYWISE!
YOUR HIGHNESS!
YOUR HIGHNESS!
YOUR MAJESTY! THE WAR IS BEGUN!
RUNCIBLE IS DEAD!
THE DRYADS IN FLAMES!
SILENCE! STOP THIS!
BUT, YOUR HIGHNESS, IT'S THE TRUTH!
IRON RAINED DOWN FROM THE SKY!
THEY'RE COMING FOR US!
THEY'RE COMING!

In this Chamber of Dreams familiar tales are retold night after night.
Story seeds are planted in the dreamer's imaginations.
And new, though recognizable, narratives blossom forth.
The stories grow, they adapt they live.
In his haste to warn the King of what had occurred, the magpie planted a seed of terror in the chamber.
Dreams became nightmares.
And in those nightmares, the witches came.

Deep beneath the ocean,
off the coast of Perrault.

‹...IF I BROKE THE WITCHES' SPELL AURORE'S HEART WOULD BE MINE AT LAST!›
‹I SAW THE PERFECT CHANCE BUT SUDDENLY CAUMONT'S TRUE QUEEN, RAPUNZEL, WAS THERE!›
‹SHE WAS SURE TO BREAK THE SPELL! SHE WAS GOING TO RUIN EVERYTHING!›
‹I RISKED ALL TO LEAD HER AWAY.›
‹WHEN I RETURNED... SOMETHING MUST HAVE CHANGED...I TRIED TO BREAK THE ENCHANT--›

‹ENOUGH OF YOUR SNIVELLING, YOU WRETCHED CREATURE.›
‹WHERE IS THE HEART?›

<I...I COULD NOT TAKE IT...>
<I TRIED...I TRIED SO HARD...HIS BLOOD IS ON THE DAGGER, SEE?>
<I...I JUST WANT TO COME HOME.>
<PLEASE... PLEASE, I...I DON'T WANT TO BE ALONE.>
<I'LL DO ANYTHING. ANYTHING. PLEASE, PLEASE JUST LET ME COME BACK.>
<YOU HAVE FAILED ME AND NOW YOU DARE TO BEG?>
<PATHETIC CREATURE!>
<COME THEN, YOU WILL NOT BE ALONE.>
<YOU WILL NEVER BE ALONE AGAIN!>

Chapter

Nightmares startled the children of Earth awake in their beds.
Tears were shed, hugs and reassurances given, and lights left on for the remainder of the dark hours.

Though they remembered little of their dreams, the fear lingered on.
Familiar places took on a sinister aspect.

They found themselves conscious of every shadow, every creaky floorboard, every door left ajar.

A distant dog's yelp became a wolf's howl, the wind in the trees a menacing whisper.
And when the night came once more, the children of Earth were reluctant to visit the realm of sleep.

For in sleep come dreams, and dreams, all too easily become nightmares.

"DO YOU FEEL IT? DO YOU FEEL THE FEAR?
"THIS WHOLE LAND TREMBLES IN TERROR OF *US!*"
NEWS OF OUR VICTORY HAS PENETRATED TO THE VERY *HEART* OF THE ENCHANTED FOREST.
NOT ONLY HAVE WE DEFEATED THE DRYADS, WE HAVE GAINED *POWER* OVER THEIR MASTERS!
WE GRANT *YOU* THIS POWER.
WE GRANT *YOU* THIS STRENGTH.
WE GRANT *YOU* THIS POWER.
WE GRANT *YOU* THIS STRENGTH.
BECOME VESSELS OF FEAR! BECOME WALKING NIGHTMARES! STRIKE TERROR INTO THE HEARTS OF ANY WHO GAZE UPON YOU!
GO FORTH! GO FORTH TO THE CENTRE OF THE FOREST! LET NOTHING STAND IN YOUR WAY!

HORSES!

LASH AND LARRUP, ONWARD GALLOP!

The Great Oak.
THE TIME HAS COME.
THE *VILLENEUVE WAR ENGINES* ARE CUTTING A PATH THROUGH THE FOREST, AND WE MUST MOVE AGAINST THEM WITH ALL THE FORCE WE CAN.
THE MACHINES *MUST* BE STOPPED, AND IF WE CANNOT DRIVE THEM BACK... WELL...
THOUGH IT PAINS ME TO SAY IT, THEN WE MUST TAKE THOSE SOLDIERS' LIVES.
YOU UNDERSTAND WHAT IS AT STAKE. THE FATE OF THIS ENTIRE WORLD RESTS WITH US!
IF THE COVEN OF WITCH-QUEENS FOUND A CLEAR COURSE TO THE GREAT OAK, THE CHAMBER OF DREAMS--
KING OBERON, YOUR HIGHNESS!

I-I AM SORRY, O' KING, NAPAIOS AND MASTER THISTLEDOWN HAVE RETURNED, YOUR MAJESTY.
GOOD NEWS! BRING THEM!
THE ARMIES OF CAUMONT AND PERRAULT WILL ARRIVE IN VILLENEUVE SOON.
THERE, THE WITCH-QUEENS WILL COMPLETE THEIR COMPACT, INCREASING THEIR POWERS THREEFOLD.
THEY'VE *ALREADY* GAINED FROM THE FEAR IN THE CHAMBER, THE SKY IS STAINED BLACK WITH IT.
BUT THEY'LL GAIN NO MORE!
TELL THE PIXIES, THE GNOMES, THE HOBS. TELL THE IMPS, THE SPRIGGANS, BOGGARTS, AND SYLPHS!
TELL THE LUBBERKIN, THE SATYRS, THE BURROW-FOLK, THE WODEWOSE!
THE HOUR OF WAR IS *HERE!*
MY KING, WE BRING GRAVE TIDINGS!
RUNCIBLE IS DEAD, SIRE.
THIS I KNOW, BROTHER NAPAIOS, SAD NEWS INDEED.
BUT YOU BRING MORE THAN NEWS. YOU TRAVEL IN THE COMPANY OF THE *LOST QUEENS!*

The Myvathen Mire.
≈SNORE≈
≈SNORE≈
SPLUSH
SPLASH

MY SISTERS AND I ARE IN A HURRY.

WE SHALL BE AT THE OAK BEFORE SUNDOWN!
THE FAE HAVE SLUNK AWAY WITH THEIR TAILS BETWEEN THEIR LEGS!
Eastern outskirts of the Enchanted Forest,
r Villeneuve.
WHERE'S YOUR MAGIC NOW, EH?
MAGIC, *HA!* WE FEAR NO MAGIC!
WE HAVE *TECHNOLOGY!*
WHAT IN THE GODS' NAMES...?
YOU, MAN! WHAT'S HAPPENING? WHY HAVE WE STOPPED?
I-I DON'T KNOW, COMMANDER SIR.

IT--IT SOUNDED LIKE THE GEARS, SIR.
BUT IT'S NOT JUST US! H-HOW IT CAN HAVE HAPPENED TO ALL THE TOWERS AT ONCE?
GREMLINS!
AAAGH! GET THEM OFF MEEEE!
KLANG

QUEEN RAPUNZEL OF CAUMONT, QUEEN TALIA OF PERRAULT, IT IS A TRUE HONOUR TO MEET YOU, YOUR MAJESTIES.
FORGIVE ME, I HAD NOT REALISED WE HAD REACHED THIS POINT IN THE STORY ALREADY.

YOUR MAJESTIES.
OUR APOLOGIES.

ERM, IT'S ALRIGHT.
BUT HOW...?

MADAME RED, I WAS VERY SORRY TO HEAR OF YOUR GRANDMOTHER'S PASSING.
OH! TH-THANK YOU. I...DON'T REALLY LIKE TO TALK ABOUT IT.

AND PRINCE HEINRICH, WHAT A HANDSOME FROG YOU MAKE, YOUR HIGHNESS.
IT ALMOST SEEMS A SHAME TO BREAK THE CURSE. STILL, THAT IS A GOOD WHILE OFF YET, EH?
HOW DO YOU KNOW THESE THINGS?

I AM OBERON. LORD OF THE ENCHANTED FOREST, *KING* OF THE FAERIES, AND GUARDIAN OF THE CHAMBER OF *DREAMS.*
EACH NIGHT MYSELF, NAPAIOS, THISTLEDOWN AND OTHERS TELL THE CHILDREN YOUR STORIES. I KNOW YOU *ALL* WELL.
COME, WE MUST HURRY.

The Kingdom of Villeneuve.
STOP THOSE HORSES!
IT'S A CAUMONT COAT OF ARMS! THAT'S KING PERSINE'S CARRIAGE!
HAIL, QUEEN BELLE.
GREETINGS, SISTERS.
IT SEEMS YOU HAVE HAD A RATHER MORE DIFFICULT JOURNEY THAN ANTICIPATED?
INDEED. THOUGH THINGS HAVE WORKED OUT FOR THE BEST, I BELIEVE.
KING AURORE AND KING PERSINE ARE GREATLY FATIGUED FROM AN HEROIC BATTLE AND WILL REQUIRE ASSISTANCE AND IMMEDIATE REST!

MY ARMIES HAVE ENGAGED THE FAE DIRECTLY. I HOPED IT MIGHT HELP DRAW THE FOREST FORCES AWAY FROM YOUR CONFLICT WITH THE DRYADS.
AH, SO YOU DO KNOW ABOUT THAT BATTLE. WE WERE NOT SURE WORD HAD GOT TO YOU...
THE ATTACK WAS SPOTTED BY A LOOKOUT. THE COMMANDER OF THE ARMY BROUGHT THE NEWS TO ME AND WE LAUNCHED OUR ASSAULT IMMEDIATELY.
NO DOUBT YOU WOULD HAVE SENT WORD YOURSELVES, YET I REGRET THAT MY CAPACITY TO RECEIVE SUCH MESSAGES HAS BECOME GREATLY DIMINISHED.
THAT IS BAD NEWS, SISTER.
INDEED.
HOWEVER, I AM HAPPY TO SAY THAT I FEEL MUCH MORE MY OLD SELF ALREADY, NOW THAT YOU ARE HERE.
SOON WE SHALL ALL BE FULLY RESTORED, EH, SISTERS?
COME CARABOSSE, COME MOTHER GOTHEL, TAKE YOUR THRONES.
THE TIME HAS COME.
OUR REIGN IS ABOUT TO BEGIN, AT LAST!

SO BELLE, THE *REAL* QUEEN BELLE, IS REALLY *HERE?*
SHE HAS BEEN WITH US FOR A WHILE NOW, YES.
BACK THERE YOU SAID *"THIS PART OF THE STORY."* WHAT STORY?
AH, THERE IS ONLY ONE STORY, QUEEN RAPUNZEL.
IT MAY BE BROKEN DOWN INTO ACTS--SOME FAVOR THREE, SOME EIGHT, SOME MANY, MANY MORE.
ITS HEROES AND VILLAINS RECAST AND REWRITTEN A THOUSAND TIMES, IT CAN BE SET MILLENNIA IN THE FUTURE, OR AEONS IN THE PAST.
BUT THE STORY ALWAYS REMAINS THE SAME.
THE STORY IS THE LAW, IS THE WORD, IS EVERYTHING. ITS RULES CANNOT BE BROKEN.

ALL RIGHT, WHAT HAPPENS NEXT, THEN?
I'M AFRAID I DO NOT KNOW.
YOU SEE, I AM NO LONGER TELLING THE TALE.
I AM A *PART* OF THE STORY NOW, JUST LIKE ALL OF YOU.

HER MAJESTY, QUEEN BELLE OF VILLENEUVE.
WE HAVE DONE OUR VERY BEST FOR HER.
BEFORE THE WITCH-QUEENS' ENCHANTMENT, SHE AND HER HUSBAND WERE GOOD FRIENDS OF THE FOREST.

Less than an hour earlier, North East of the Great Oak.

WHAT IS IT?
WHAT DO YOU SEE, DÁINN?

THE CLUMSY TREAD OF HUMANS. *MANY* HUMANS, DÁINN SAYS.
LET US *MEET* THEM WITH OUR *HORNS*, BROTHERS.

CHAARRGE!

"BY THE GODS, WHAT IS THAT LIGHT?"
"WOAH! STEADY, DUNEYRR! *STEADY!*"
"THEIR *FACES!*"

"THEIR FACES!"
"I NEVER FELT SUCH...SUCH TERROR."

IF IT HADN'T BEEN FOR DÁINN...IF I'D LOST MY GRIP ON HIM...
IF I'D HAD TO LOOK INTO THOSE EYES FOR A MOMENT LONGER, I THINK I'D...I'D HAVE GONE MAD.

COURAGE, MY BROTHER. STAY STRONG.
FOR, IF WHAT YOU SAY IS TRUE, I FEAR WE MAY HAVE TO LOOK UPON THEM TOGETHER ALL TOO SOON.

LISTEN, I'M SORRY, BUT WE CAN'T GET CAUGHT UP IN THIS...
I NEED TO GET TO MY HUSBAND AND BREAK HIS ENCHANTMENT.
IF I CAN GET TO VILLENEUVE, I CAN BREAK MOTHER GOTHEL'S SPELL.
THAT'LL HELP YOU, TOO, RIGHT?

YES. YES, OF COURSE.
AND I THINK I HAVE AN IDEA OF HOW TO DO IT.

WE WYRD SISTERS, WITCHES THREE, ARE MET THIS DAY FOR SORCERY. HAIL, SISTERS, AND WELL MET.

THRICE TO THINE, AND THRICE TO MINE, AND THRICE AGAIN, TO MAKE UP NINE.

WE WYRD SISTERS, HAND IN HAND, RULERS O'ER ALL THIS LAND, MAKE THE MAGIC MARK LIKE SO.

I, WITCH GOTHEL, OF THE DOORLESS TOWER.
I, WITCH CARABOSSE, OF THE ACCURSED NEEDLE.
I, WITCH BELLADONNA, THE LOVER SCORNED.
WE WYRD SISTERS, COVEN OF THREE, UNITE WITH THEE, AND THEE. AND THEE. IT IS DONE!
AH, FEEL THE POWER, SISTERS.
THE COMPACT IS COMPLETE.
INDEED.
I FEEL STRONGER ALREADY.

The streets of Villeneuve.

ACH! YOU STUPID BEAST!

I'LL HAVE TO FETCH-- OH!

HISSSSH

MONSTERS!
RUN FOR YOUR LIVES!

"THEY'RE COMING FROM THE WATER!"
"THEY'RE IN THE SEWERS, EVEN THE WELLS!"
"THE LAKE! MY GODS, LOOK AT THE LAKE!"
"THEY'RE EVERYWHERE!"

FETCH THE WATCH! THE ARMY!
THERE IS NONE! THEY'RE FIGHTING IN THE FOREST!
SAVE YOURSELVES!
GET INSIDE!
AAAGH! GODS HELP ME!
THERE'S TOO MANY OF 'EM!

WE'RE HERE.

THE WHOLE CITY IS FULL OF *MERMAIDS.*
THEY'RE EVERYWHERE!
AH, SO THAT WOULD ACCOUNT FOR ALL THE COMMOTION AND THE *JUMPING.*

BUT *MERMAIDS?* WHAT ARE THEY DOING *HERE?*

I DON'T KNOW, AND I DON'T REALLY CARE.
THERE'S NO TIME.

OUCH, MY BACK! NEXT TIME WE MAGICALLY DISGUISE OURSELVES AS A HORSE, I THINK I WOULD LIKE TO BE THE *HEAD.*
WHAT NOW, RAPA?

NOW WE FIND MY HUSBAND.
AND GODS HELP THE WITCH THAT GETS IN MY WAY.

Chapter

"SISTERS, WE ARE ALMOST THERE! SOON THIS WORLD WILL BE OURS!
"BELLE, YOUR LOYAL SOLDIERS WILL BE ALMOST AT THE GREAT OAK.
"THE PATH CUT BY THEIR INGENIOUS CONTRAPTIONS WILL ENABLE US TO WALK IN, UNHAMPERED.
"THE COMBINED FORCES OF MIGHTY CAUMONT AND GREAT PERRAULT HAVE LAUNCHED THEIR SURPRISE ATTACK FROM THE NORTHEAST.
"THE SPELL WE CAST--THE POWER OF THE FEAR--WILL MAKE THEIR JOURNEY A SWIFT AND CEASELESS ONE.
"OUR ARMIES WILL MEET AT THE GREAT OAK, AND CRUSH WHAT RESISTANCE OBERON AND HIS FLOWER FAERIES CAN MUSTER.
"IT SHALL BE DONE IN AN INSTANT. THEIR FLUTTERING WINGS GROUND BENEATH OUR BOOTS.
"ONLY THEN SHALL THE OAK GIVE UP ITS *SECRETS...* AND ITS POWER."

THERE, IN THE CHAMBER OF DREAMS, WE SHALL WRITE A NEW CHAPTER. ONE OF DARKNESS.
OH, TO SEE THE FAERIE KING COWED!
OBERON HAS LONG BEEN A THORN IN OUR SIDE.
WE SHALL PLUCK THAT THORN TODAY! AND THEN, WHAT JOY!
INDEED. WE SHOULD MAKE HASTE.
WAIT, WHAT *IS* THAT NOISE?
AND THAT *SMELL*...
IT SEEMS YOU HAVE VISITORS, BEL-- SHE'S GONE!
OBERON MUST BE FEARFUL INDEED, TO THROW HIS LOT IN WITH THESE *THINGS!*
IT MATTERS NOT, WE HAVE THE POWER OF THE COMPACT!
CEASE YOUR PRATTLE, YOU PAINTED *CRONES!*
WE ARE NOT HERE FROM THE ELVEN KING.

WHY ARE YOU HERE, THEN? NO. DON'T TELL ME. YOU'LL BE DEAD SOON ANYWAY.
FZZZZT
PLEASE DON'T TRY THAT AGAIN. YOU WILL MAKE US ANGRY.
WE COULD KILL YOU ALL!
PAH! YOUR MAGIC HURTS US LESS THAN IT DOES THE FAE.
AND YOU USE A HUMAN ARMY TO FIGHT THEM, DON'T YOU?
WHAT IS IT THAT YOU WANT?
OH, I THOUGHT YOU WOULD NEVER ASK.
WE ARE HERE FOR KING AURORE.

KLIK
YOU WOULD RELEASE ME. WHY? WHY NOW? IT'S BEEN SO LONG. SO MANY YEARS IN THESE CHAINS.
BECAUSE, MY LOVE, YOUR WAIT IS OVER. TODAY YOU WILL BE A BEAST NO LONGER. TODAY I SHALL DELIVER YOU TO REDEMPTION BY THE SIMPLE POWER OF A KISS.
TODAY WE SHALL RETURN TO THE THRONE AS MAN AND WIFE, AND RULE OUR PEOPLE TOGETHER.
I-I DO NOT UNDERSTAND. HOW CAN THIS BE? WHERE HAVE YOU BEEN...ALL THESE YEARS?
IT DOES NOT MATTER, BELOVED, I AM HERE NOW. YOUR OWN SWEET BELLE RETURNED TO YOU ONCE MORE.
COME, HOLD ME, KISS ME AND SHED THIS LUMPEN FORM FOREVER.

LIARRR!
"LUMPEN FORM"? A MONSTER FOR FRIGHTENING CHILDREN?!
IS THAT WHAT I AM?
I-I DID NOT--
YOU COME, AS MY LOST LOVE, MY SAVIOUR, MY REDEMPTION, BUT YOUR CONTEMPT FOR THIS GRACELESS SHELL DRIPS FROM EVERY PORE.
I PITY YOU, WITCH. THAT ALL YOUR ART CANNOT DISGUISE YOUR OWN WRETCHED SOUL.
I-I LOVE YOU... PLEASE...
SILENCE! IT IS NOT LOVE WHICH KEPT ME HERE IN CHAINS. IT IS NOT LOVE WHICH SOUGHT TO TRICK ME!
I AM NOT SOME CREATURE WHICH CAN BE OWNED!
COULD YOU STAND IT? ALL THESE YEARS OF TORMENT? OF PAIN? WHAT WOULD YOU DO IF YOU WERE ME?
WOULD YOU TAKE PLEASURE IN DESTROYING THE SOURCE OF ALL YOUR SUFFERING? WOULD YOU KILL THEM?
I COULD NOT BLAME YOU IF YOU DID SO, BUT BEFORE YOU DO, GRANT ME ONE THING.
LET ME TELL YOU THE TRUTH, FOR ONCE AND ALL.

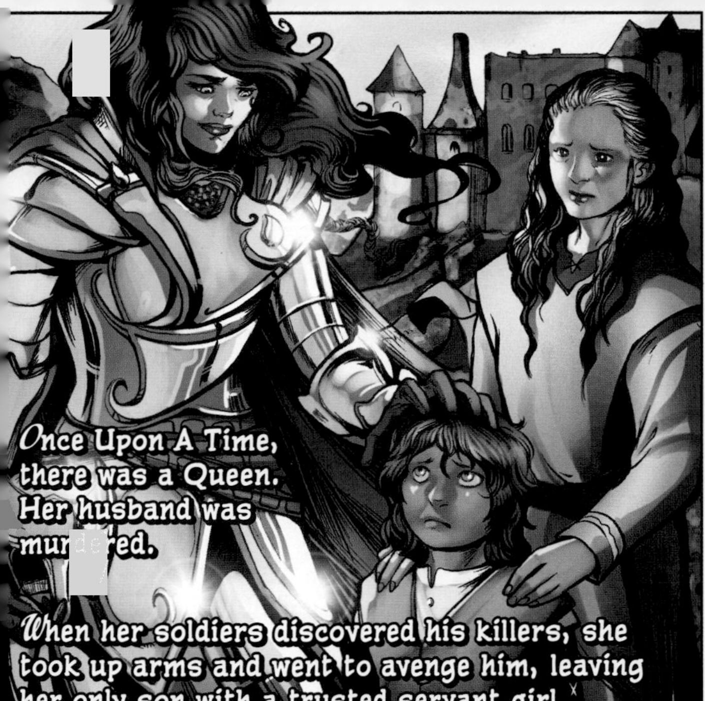

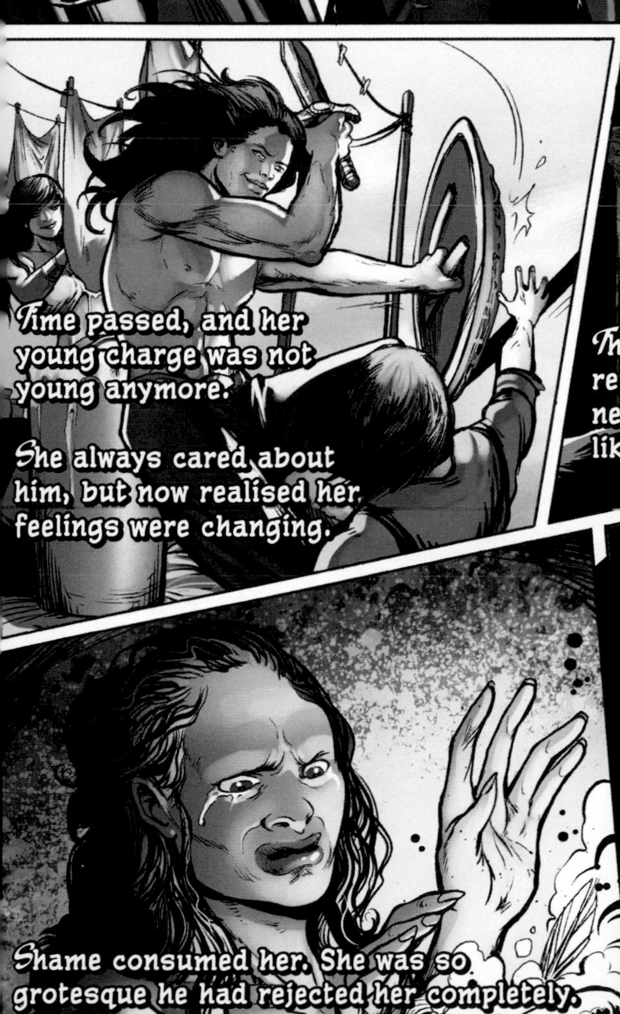

One night, she told him. She longed to be his wife, not his guardian.

The Prince was repulsed. He could never think of her like that!

Shame consumed her. She was so grotesque he had rejected her completely.

But she was also a witch, and so she cast a spell.

"If I cannot have you, no-one shall! Live your days in this lumpen form, a monster to terrify children!

"A monster you'll remain, unlovable, until this spell be broken with a kiss."

one hundred years, the Prince lived alone in the castle, pacing the corridors night and day.
He was grotesque, unlovable. He was a monster with no hope of that magical kiss.
But of course love often finds a way, even in unlikely circumstances.
A young Merchant's daughter by the name of Belle, fell in love with him, and broke the spell.
WHEN GOTHEL SUGGESTED WE STEAL THE KINGDOMS BY IMPERSONATING THEIR QUEENS, I THOUGHT I HAD ANOTHER CHANCE.
WE WOULD BE TOGETHER AT LAST.
BUT MY OWN SPELL REVERTED, AND YOU WERE A BEAST ONCE MORE.
WHERE IS SHE?
"WE SET THEM TO WANDER, SHUNNED BY ALL THEY MET. THEY WOULD NOT REMEMBER ANYTHING, AND WOULD NOT KNOW WHO THEY WERE.
"I... I DO NOT KNOW WHAT HAS BECOME OF HER..."
BELLE!
I'M COMING FOR YOU, BELLE!

THWIP
IT WILL NOT HOLD THEM LONG, BUT MAY BUY US A LITTLE MORE TIME.
THIS ENCHANTED ARMY, THEY'RE COMING FOR QUEEN BELLE, RIGHT? CAN SHE NOT BE MOVED?
NO, THEY ARE NOT COMING FOR THE QUEEN, THEY COME FOR THE CHAMBER OF DREAMS.
AT THE HEART OF THIS WORLD STANDS THE GREAT OAK, AND AT ITS HEART IS THE CHAMBER OF DREAMS.
EACH NIGHT WE TELL STORIES IN THE CHAMBER.
AND EACH NIGHT, THE DREAMERS WITHIN *DREAM* OUR WORLD INTO EXISTENCE.
RAPA SAID WHEN SHE WAS IN GOTHEL'S TOWER, THE WITCH TOOK POWER FROM HER DREAMS.
IF THEY GOT TO THE CHAMBER... ALL THOSE CHILDREN!

AND WHAT IF SHE DOESN'T?
WE CAN STILL BEAT THIS ARMY OF FEAR, RIGHT?
ALL WE CAN DO NOW IS TRY TO KEEP THE ARMY OF FEAR AT BAY AND HOPE THAT QUEEN RAPUNZEL... RAPA AS SHE IS NOW... CAN *BREAK* THE ENCHANTMENT.
I DO NOT KNOW.
TRULY, I DO NOT KNOW.
I WANT TO SEE THIS CHAMBER OF DREAMS FOR MYSELF, I HAVE AN IDEA THAT MIGHT--
WAIT. JUST A MOMENT.
I HAVE TO GO, MY LOVE. THERE'S GOT TO BE A WAY...
YOU UNDERSTAND, DON'T YOU?
TAKE CARE, LOVE. THAT'S ALL. TAKE CARE.

IS IT NOT LOVE? THEN WHY DO I FEEL THIS PAIN? THIS AGONY?
I HAVE DAMNED THIS WORLD JUST TO KISS HIS LIPS, TO FEEL HIS EMBRACE.
I, BELLADONNA, THE LOVER SCORNED. PAH!
WHAT HAVE I DONE? WHAT HAVE I DONE?
HKK
RAPUNZEL... YOU SURVIVED.
LONGER THAN YOU, WITCH!
I AM... DYING, THEN. THE PACT...AND THE ENCHANTMENT, IS BROKEN.
THE KINGS... ARE IN THE... WEST TOWER.
THE OTHERS... GOTHEL... CARABOSSE... THEY WILL WEAKEN NOW.
SWEAR...
...SWEAR TO ME...SWEAR THAT YOU WILL...
...KILL THEM, TOO...

OH, I SWEAR IT!
"I'LL MAKE THEM PAY."
COME ON, HEINRICH.
WE'VE GOT TO GET TO THE TOWER.

...SHE TASTED THE PORRIDGE OF THE MIDDLE BEAR, AND THAT WAS TOO COLD FOR HER, SO SHE SAID A BAD WORD ABOUT THAT, TOO.
SO THEN SHE WENT TO THE PORRIDGE OF THE LITTLE BEAR.
DID THE BEARS CATCH HER, AND EAT HER UP?
DID A MONSTER COME OUT OF THE WOODS?
"WHAT? NO! THERE ARE NO MONSTERS IN THIS STORY!"
THERE'S NOTHING TO BE AFRAID OF!
NO, THAT ISN'T TRUE.
SO, THESE ARE THE DREAMERS?
YOU CAN'T JUST LIE TO THEM. IT'S NOT GOING TO HELP ANYTHING.

"THERE ARE MONSTERS. THERE ARE WITCHES.
"AND THEY'RE COMING THIS WAY."
NO, YOU CAN'T--
I MUST! CAN'T YOU SEE?
MY NAME IS TALIA. I USED TO BE A PRINCESS.
IN FACT, I USED TO BE A QUEEN.
"I'M THE LITTLE GIRL WHO SLEPT FOR A HUNDRED YEARS.
"THE WITCHES TRIED TO ROB ME OF MY HAPPILY EVER AFTER.
"ME, AND OTHERS LIKE ME."

KRAK
PERSINE!
WHO IS THERE?
PERSINE.
OH, PERSINE.
OH, MY LOVE, I'M HERE.
IT'S ME.
IT'S RAPUNZEL.
RAPUNZEL, MY LOVE?
YOUR HAIR...YOU'VE CHANGED IT.

YOU LOOK MORE BEAUTIFUL THAN EVER.
YOU!
YOU'RE SUPPOSED TO BE DEAD!

"DID YOU EVER FEEL LIKE YOU HAD NO CONTROL OVER ANYTHING?"
LIKE YOU WERE JUST A CHARACTER IN A STORY WHOSE ENDING WAS ALREADY WRITTEN?
WELL, THAT'S JUST HOW I FELT FOR A LONG TIME.
"BUT THOSE WITCHES *CHANGED* MY STORY.
"THEY STOLE MY LIFE AWAY, PRETENDED TO BE ME SO THAT THEY COULD GET TO THIS PLACE.
"TO GET TO YOU.
"BECAUSE THEY WANT--THEY *NEED*--YOU TO BE AFRAID.
"YOUR FEAR IS *EVERYTHING* TO THEM.
"THEIR MAGIC IS FUELLED BY YOUR NIGHTMARES.
"BUT YOU DON'T *NEED* TO BE AFRAID!"

"THE MONSTERS ARE ONLY FRIGHTENING IF *YOU* ALLOW THEM TO BE.

"THE WITCHES ONLY HAVE POWER IF *YOU* GIVE IT TO THEM.

"THIS IS *YOUR* STORY, *YOUR* DREAM.

"IT'S UP TO *YOU* WHAT HAPPENS NEXT.

Their bodies ached from their ceaseless march, and their minds stung from the wickedness that had clouded them for so long.
OBERON!
IS SHE HERE?
YOUR MAJESTY, IT HAS BEEN--
IS SHE HERE?
YES.
QUEEN BELLE IS HERE.
THEN TAKE ME TO HER.

SHE COULD NOT COME TO ME. I UNDERSTAND THAT NOW.
I KNEW SHE WOULD SEEK YOU OUT.
I AM GLAD SHE...HAD *SOMEONE* TO TURN TO.
I KNOW WHAT THERE WAS BETWEEN YOU.
BUT *I* AM HER TRUE LOVE. AND I AM FREE AGAIN NOW.
YOUR HIGHNESS, YOU SPEAK OF THINGS LONG PAST. THINGS WHICH I... I...
I FEAR THAT ALL IS NOT AS YOU IMAGINE IT TO BE.
AT LEAST I KNOW YOU WILL BELIEVE THAT I HAVE DONE ALL I CAN FOR HER. AND FOR YOU.

AH, THAT HANDSOME FACE.
I DO NOT PART WITH HIM *LIGHTLY.*
TALI--*OH!* WH-WHO ARE YOU?
WHAT'S THE MATTER DEAR? DON'T YOU--
HEKATE! M-MY HANDS, MY BEAUTIFUL HANDS!
ALL GONE... THESE WITHERED CLAWS REMAIN!
VILE! HATEFUL FLESH TO HANG FROM MY BONES LIKE THIS!
NO! HELP ME! ***HELP ME!***
WE ARE UNDONE! THE SPELL HAS BEEN BROKEN!
ALL IS LOST!

LIKE A NIGHTMARE, ISN'T IT? AND IN A TOWER, TOO!
ONLY THIS TIME, IT'S YOUR NIGHTMARE!
THWAK
HOLD, MY KING. RAPA MUST DO THIS ALONE.
SHE HAS WAITED A LONG TIME FOR THIS. LET US NOT DENY HER IT NOW.
YOU'VE LOST! YOUR SPELL IS BROKEN!
I HAVE BEATEN YOU!
AND NOW I, THE LITTLE GIRL YOU HELD PRISONER FOR ALL THOSE YEARS, WILL END THIS ONCE AND FOR ALL!
NOW CHILD, IS THAT ANY WAY TO SPEAK TO YOUR DEAR OLD MOTHER GOTHEL?
FOOOOM

OH, BELLE, MY LOVE. MY ONLY LOVE.
I AM HERE.
I HAVE COME FOR YOU.
AWAKEN, MY QUEEN.

The touch of his true love's lips soothed the savage beast within, and once again King Beauregard of Villeneuve's aged curse was lifted.
Queen Belle's enchanted too was broken with that kiss.
But she, tragically, was far beyond waking.
Belle wandered as the other banished Queen did. Her memories all but obliterated, cursed to be shunned wherever she went.
Somehow she made her way into the Enchanted Forest but by the time the faerie folk found her, she had already passed.
Knowing that Belle's love was the only thing that could break Beauregard's enchantment. Oberon cast a powerful spell to keep her as she was.
Alas, the sands of time cannot be stopped forever.

KADOOM!
YOU WILL PAY FOR WHAT YOU HAVE DONE! YOU WILL PAY!
GOTHEL!
SILENCE, WITCH! STAY WHERE YOU ARE!
UNGRATEFUL BRAT!
DIDN'T I RAISE YOU? KEEP YOU SAFE FOR ALL THOSE YEARS, BEFORE HE CAME ALONG?
DIDN'T I TELL YOU WONDERFUL STORIES EVERY NIGHT?
YOU REMEMBER THOSE STORIES.
DON'T YOU?

HA-HA-HA-HA!
RAPUNZEL, RAPUNZEL, WITH HER LOVELY LONG HAIR, RAPUNZEL, RAPUNZEL SO *EASY* TO *SCARE!*
N-N-NO. N-NO, PLEASE. NO. NO!
COME, SISTER CARABOSSE.
I AM READY, GOTHEL!
FAREWELL, RAPUNZEL, WE SHALL MEET AGAIN SOON, I HAVE NO DOUBT.
UNTIL THEN, I SHALL SEE YOU IN YOUR *NIGHTMARES,* CHILD!
HA HA HA HA HA HA HA HA HA HA HA

The next day, King Beauregard spoke to the gathered people of the Three Kingdoms and Enchanted Forest.
A great evil had been done to them, and their minds had been clouded with dark magic.
But the spells were broken and curses lifted, thanks to Queens Talia and Rapunzel.
There was cheering and rejoicing, but then he grew stern.
Though one witch--whose name he could not speak--lay dead, two more escaped.
And Aurore, his brother King, was kidnapped, who knows where.
Caumont and Perrault may still be in the witches thrall.
If some witch took their fallen sister's place, the rite of three could be repeated.
Yes, a great battle had been won, but the war might only be beginning.